# STAND IN YOUR POWER

A Guide to Becoming the Most Aligned and Empowered
Version of Yourself

MARY-THERESA TRINGALE

# Contents

*This book is dedicated to the ladies of*
*The Aligned & Empowered Project—*
*especially my OG's:*
*Jo, Lilly, Kate, Alecia, Laura, Liz, and Kelly.*

*Thank you for helping me turn grief into an opportunity to*
*STAND IN OUR POWER, together.*

"If you're serious about changing your life, you'll find a way. If you're not, you'll find an excuse."
—Jen Sincero, *You Are a Badass*

# Introduction

Hi ya, I'm Mary-Theresa Tringale (pronounced Tring-gal-lee, it's Italian!) and my friends call me Mary or M-T. Please feel free to do the same!

I'm an accountability and high-performance coach and founder of the group coaching program, The Aligned & Empowered Project (AEP).

Currently, I live in Portland, Maine, by way of NYC, by way of Boston, which is where I grew up (hometown Billerica, pronounced Bill-ric-ca), but I spent much of my childhood walking the mean streets of Beacon Hill and Park Street on Sundays after church. I went to Emerson College, also located in Boston, and I work full-time (at the time of writing this book) for a kick-ass nonprofit called WinterKids as the events and sponsorships manager.

This book is a tribute to the lessons, practices, and tools I used in my personal journey to feeling empowered and finding alignment in my life so that I could truly STAND IN MY POWER the way I was born to.

In short, this book is the blueprint I used to bring me back to life at a time when I felt the most lost and out of control I had ever experienced.

In spring of 2019, my family and I got devastating news. My father, Domenic, who had been dealing with health issues since he was first diagnosed with cancer in 1992, had a brain infection—the second in three months—and his skull was porous. There was officially nothing more doctors could do.

At the end of April, he was sent home with "hours to days" to live. The doctors didn't even think he would make it from Boston to Maine. But make it he did. Not just to Maine, and not just through those hours. Days turned into weeks, weeks turned into months, and suddenly it seemed like he would be living this way forever.

My dad had developed dementia-like symptoms, which meant he couldn't be left alone for even a minute. This meant we (my two brothers and I) were on call for support at all times.

This was the ultimate feeling of "out of control" I had ever experienced in my thirty-six years of living. Every day was a mystery; we couldn't plan or assume one way or another. Any day, any time, our world with my dad living in it could come to an end. He was a ticking time bomb, and all we could do was wait.

I'm sure you know the saying, "When it rains, it pours." Welp, this was the truth of my life at the time.

Personally, I was falling apart inside and out. My life wasn't exactly the dream life I had envisioned for myself at thirty-six. My business wasn't thriving the way I had hoped, I was struggling financially, and I was out of shape and plain-old miserable. It felt like no matter what I did, I couldn't get out of my own way. It was always one step forward and eighteen steps back.

At the end of May I had a total meltdown on the floor of my bedroom, crying and venting via voice memo to my business coach Sarah about how I didn't know how to move forward. Between what was happening with my dad and what was happening in my life personally, I just felt like I was in a total downward spiral, and it was all a really bad time for everything to be happening all at once.

Luckily, I had a conference coming up called THRIVE: Make Money Matter in Las Vegas. It was a conference I had booked before my dad got sick, and with my mother's blessing, I went to Las Vegas with a goal to be open and receive whatever came my way.

Well, the conference changed my life. You'll learn later in this book how, but the biggest impact came when I heard about this program created by entrepreneur Andy Frisella called 75 Hard.

75 Hard is, as Andy calls it, a mindset and discipline program. You have five tasks you must do every day, without failure, for seventy-five days. If you miss one thing, you have to start over from the beginning.

Tasks include:

- Working out two times a day for forty-five minutes minimum, once being outside—no matter what
- Drinking a gallon of water
- Following a diet, no alcohol
- Reading ten pages of a nonfiction, self-improvement book

- Taking a progress picture

What intrigued me most about this program was that everyone was talking about how hard it was to do it. Andy challenged every person in the room to try it, predicting that no one would actually be able to do it completely.

Challenge accepted.

In my old life, I was the master of taking on physical challenges that seemed impossible.

When I lived in New York City, I trained for four Olympic Distance Triathlons with Team in Training. Somehow, I managed to stick to the training schedule despite my incredibly demanding job in magazine publishing. I was disciplined, I was in incredible shape, I was committed, and I loved every minute.

Unfortunately, in 2012 I injured my back and dealt with a case of hives (due to a microscopic parasite) that sidelined me and caused me to gain thirty pounds due to the steroids I was on.

In 2019, at thirty-six, I had yet to find my way back to the disciplined athlete I had been when I was training for races.

I felt lost and out of control. I needed something to get me back in line with who I used to be, who I felt I was born to be.

So, I bit the bullet and I committed to 75 Hard. On June 11, 2019, I started Day 1 of my first round of 75 Hard. I decided with my entire body and soul that nothing would stop me from finishing it without failure the first time around. (I have since completed Andy's entire LIVE

HARD program and done four additional rounds of 75 Hard).

I had zero expectations of what this journey was going to give me. I just knew that I was at the lowest point of my life yet, and the only way out was up (and through).

Words can't completely describe what working this program wholeheartedly did for me. At a minimum, it allowed me to find my way back to being disciplined and an athlete again.

At a higher level, it connected me to my inner wisdom in a way I had never known before.

I learned the healing powers of nature from walking every day, I gained knowledge in mindset and manifestation and empowerment from the books I read, and I learned about boundaries and communicating for success.

I started to discover what I was truly made of and how if I believed in myself, anything was possible—and how I could literally do anything I put my mind to.

I also learned how even on the hardest days, like the final days of my dad's life, I could still choose me above all else in order to serve those around me at my highest capacity.

On days 52, 53, 54, and 55 of my first round of 75 Hard, my dad's brain infection finally took over his body. My mother, brothers, and I were his full-time care until finally, he was able to go into hospice.

Each day, I clearly communicated with my family what I needed to get my habits done on those days, keeping my commitment to myself my number 1 priority.

I was kind and clear with my asks, and they were able to give me the space and time I needed to fulfill them.

Then, because each day I filled my cup first, I was able to be there for my family as my best self until the time finally came for my dad to pass on.

My dad's passing was something we had anticipated for years. But just because we had been waiting for it didn't mean it wasn't hard. I know for sure if I hadn't been on the journey with 75 Hard, I probably wouldn't have been able to handle his death with as much grace.

It was not a joyous occasion by any means, but during it, I was able to find gratitude and relief knowing that his suffering had finally come to an end. I know that I was able to be clearheaded, aligned, and grounded in the experience of his death because of the inner work I had been doing up to that point.

I finished up my first round of 75 Hard at the end of August and proceeded to maintain a lifestyle of commitment to habits, alignment, and STANDING IN MY POWER.

I shared every step of my journey on social media and welcomed the incredible support I received from friends, family, and people I hadn't spoken to in years (or ever!).

I continued down the path of building a side business focused on events while maintaining my full-time job. And still after all this deep work, I had a sense that I wasn't fully aligned in allowing myself to be the person I was meant to be.

In February of 2020, I heard the whisper, the one that had been trying to get my attention for months up to this point.

It was a whisper that told me I was coaching the wrong thing. That event coaching truly wasn't where I was meant to be, that I was meant to help guide others along a similar journey that I had been through using habits, mindset, and self-discovery.

So I took a leap. I joined the digital business coaching program E+mpower lead by my friend and business mentor Jess (Glazer) DeRose and again opened myself up to receive whatever came my way.

What came my way was magic, and it was called The Aligned & Empowered Project (AEP).

What I had been ignoring for months was all the people who had been following my journey who were now asking me for advice and insight as to how I got there. Not only did I look *good*, but (as I was told) I was also "*glowing.*" Could I help them do the same?

When COVID-19 first hit, I started a seven-day walking challenge group on Facebook. I knew that walking every day for forty-five minutes or more, no matter what, was the number 1 habit that helped me learn to thrive again. I wanted to help others create this impactful habit in their own lives too.

I did the challenge, held people accountable, and cele-brated every day along the way. It was incredible. The biggest piece of feedback I heard was how grateful people were for the accountability, and I knew in that moment, I was an Accountability Coach.

I created the concept for The Aligned & Empowered Project as a combo of what I had experienced with 75 Hard (The AEP is *not* the 75 Hard program), the lessons I learned in the books I read, and the support (both from community and coaching) that I had while I was going through my own transformation.

I pitched the program to my small community on Instagram and Facebook, and magically, seven incredible women said *yes* to giving it a go. The Aligned & Empowered Project was officially born. (Side note, The AEP is specifically for women, but I do coach anyone as a one-on-one client and we walk through these processes and steps outlined in this book).

Ever since, my life has been nothing short of a dream. I've had countless opportunities to continue to support both women and men as they work to change their lives for the better, I've had the chance to be a support coach and guest coach in other programs, and I have a vision for my business and the life I want to live after leave WinterKids for a life of full-time entrepreneurship in the second half of 2022.

This book is dedicated to those seven women who said yes to me, my dream, and to finding their way to standing in their power way back in April of 2020.

The chapters that follow are the tools, tips, practices, and perspectives I use to guide my clients through The Aligned & Empowered Project process. These resources have helped five rounds of women (and possibly more by the time you read this) understand their limiting beliefs, rewrite their stories, take aligned action, and ultimately learn how to STAND IN THEIR POWER to have the life of their dreams.

The journey for them all continues, and same for me. This book is where we start time and again when we may have lost our way and need to find our way back to remembering who the hell we are.

Please take what works for you and leave the rest. Revisit when you need to, and share this book with others who might find it helpful in their own lives.

I look forward to cheering you on as you commit to this journey so you, too, can feel empowered and aligned and find your way to STANDING IN YOUR POWER.

xo

M-T

# ONE

# Be-Do-Have

"Only when you explore the ecstasy of simply being,
where even to breathe is a distraction,
can you call yourself complete."
—Sadghuru

## WHERE ARE ALL MY "DOERS" AT?

RAISE YOUR HAND IF YOU THINK YOU CAN "DO" YOUR WAY into success.

Raise your hand if you have ever thought, "Starting tomorrow, I'm going to work out every day, eat only fruits and vegetables, and drink only water in order to have the body of my dreams."

Raise your hand if you have ever believed that the only way to get the big paycheck is to out-perform (or out-do) your competition.

Raise your hand if you think the only way to be the perfect fill-in-the-blank (mother, wife, daughter, student, employee, etc.) is to do all the things expected of you, perfectly.

Whether you raised your hand for one or all the above, I am with you. I see you. I feel you. And I am here to give you permission to *lean into another way*.

I lived for a very long time with a belief system that agreed with you: in order to *have it all*, I had to *do it all*, and *then* I would be: *confident, successful, happy, peaceful, etc*.

I believed to my core the only order was:

1. DO
2. HAVE
3. BE

- *In order to be skinny*, I had to work out non-stop and eat perfectly, and then I would be confident.
- *In order to have a romantic relationship*, I had to do things to impress him to show my value, and then I would receive love and support.
- *In order to have financial abundance*, I had to out-perform my competition, and then I would be financially free.
- *In order to have the home, clothes, décor, car, etc. I desired*, I had to hustle until I was burned out, and then I would find joy in the every-day.

I had no clue that I was "doing" it in the wrong order.

The real order, the one that creates change and impact and opportunity, is:

1. BE
2. DO
3. HAVE

This particular lesson was one I had to hear multiple times, from multiple resources, before it really landed and stuck, becoming one of those "Aha!" moments Oprah is always talking about.

The moment came in June 2019 during a Money Mindset workshop with my mindset coach, Nick Pags.

My intention for taking the workshop was out of alignment with the BE-DO-HAVE process.

I was there because I had been working hard "doing" all the things I needed to do to start my business and building The Aligned & Empowered Project, but I felt I wasn't "having" the results I desired. I wanted to learn from Nick how I could "do" better.

I was there because the DO-HAVE-BE process I had been living in was—shocker—not working.

Even though I had been a student of mindset work for nearly two years and a student of Nick's for about four months, I still hadn't understood how I had it all backwards and that I was blocking my own potential.

I was my own biggest obstacle.

And again, on this particular day, after four intensive hours learning about how to rewire my mindset around money, the first question I asked during Q&A was focused on *doing*.

I raised my little yellow virtual hand and asked:

"Nick, I have been working my ass off for years trying to become a successful entrepreneur, *but I'm still not rich AF.* What am I *doing* wrong?"

Nick replied, exasperated: "Mary, I'm hearing a *whole lot of doing* and not enough *being!* We all know you are the queen of doing—you can do the shit out of anything—but how are you *being* the person you want to be?"

I was *stunned* to silence (which is saying *a lot* for me). I stared back at him across the screen, finally hearing the message I needed to hear for years.

I had completely missed the entire point of the workshop.

I had been physically present, but with blinders on, only ready to receive the messages that filled my narrative of DO-HAVE-BE.

Have you ever done the exercise where you take fifteen seconds, look around the room you are in, and look for all the red things in the room; and then you are asked to close your eyes and list all the blue things in the room? Generally, you can't list the blue things because you were laser focused on the items that were red, and nothing else mattered.

That was me in this workshop and in life. Always only paying attention to how I DO life, and never allowing myself to dream about who and how I wanted to BE.

I now realized I had to start with *who did I want to BE?* And then figure out the aligned and inspired action behind that beingness in order to have it all (or as close to it as possible).

But I was still stuck. And perhaps you, too, might still be a bit confused by this whole **BE-DO-HAVE** silliness.

Once I got through my *shock* to Nick's spot-on assessment of where I was in that moment, I was able to ask the only question I had—one that I hear more often than not from others doing this work.

Perhaps this is the question you have right now too.

I asked, "I don't get it, how do I *do* being?"

We both laughed at the irony of the question, but I also would like to acknowledge how valid of a question it is.

And so, my journey to discovering the answer to this question began …

What I didn't realize at the time is that I had already begun to work on answering this question through my own journey. I just wasn't aware of it.

## WHO DO YOU WANT TO BE?

Steve Jobs famously said, "You can't connect the dots looking forward; you can only connect them looking backward. So you have to trust that the dots will somehow connect in your future. You have to trust in something—your gut, destiny, life, karma, whatever."

This quote couldn't be more true for my journey, and perhaps yours too.

As I've had several opportunities over the years to look back and connect my own dots, I see now that my entire journey happened because I was *very* clear on who I wanted to be.

When I began the 75 Hard journey, I wanted to be someone who was disciplined, focused, and an athlete again.

If I dig even deeper, I wanted to find myself again. I wanted to have no excuses. I wanted to be extraordinary. I wanted to feel *good*.

And, most importantly, I wanted to be someone who didn't let *anything* get in the way of having these things.

What I didn't know at the time was how this clear sense of being would keep me dedicated to my mission and how the commitment to staying consistent with these habits would ultimately change my life forever.

One of my favorite books I've read on this journey has been *Atomic Habits* by James Clear. This book has been an essential tool in helping me understand why my journey of transformation and implementing habits into my life was so successful and how it may not be as impactful for others.

In *Atomic Habits*, Clear explains how in making habits stick, we should be focused on connecting the habits to our identity instead of connecting habits to our goals.

Clear notes that while goals are good, we are often not connected to them internally, and they generally have an end date, not allowing them to ever become part of us.

## FOR EXAMPLE:

Let's say you have a goal of running a marathon. In my experience, this is generally how the process goes:

1. You commit to the goal: running a marathon
2. You DO all the things to get you there (follow a

training program, find groups to run with, sacrifice Friday night parties for a good Saturday morning run, eat better than usual, stretch and rest more often, etc.)

3. You run the marathon, cross the finish line, and celebrate!
4. You never run another mile again (or close to it).

Raise your hand if the above sounds familiar. Yeah, me too.

That is, until I started prioritizing *being* above all else.

When you begin with identifying *who you want to be*, you are creating a strong and undeniable *why*.

*"When you know your* why *you can endure any how."*—Victor Frankl

So, let's try this again. This time, we answer the question "Who do I want to BE?".

We'll use the running/marathon example again but different this time:

**BE:**

Question: Who do you want to BE?

Answer: Someone who is a fit and healthy runner.

**DO:**

Question: What actions can you DO to help you be this person?

Answer(s):

- Move your body every day (run three to four times a week, stretch or active recovery on other days)
- Keep a journal of your mental journey to discover growth and work through mental blocks
- Start meal planning so you are sure you are fueling your body accordingly
- Get a support system (running club, coach, training partner, etc.)

## HAVE:

HAVING means receiving, and eventually, because your daily habits had nothing to do with a goal but rather your way of BEING, running becomes *part* of you. You'll start to receive the benefits of becoming the person you always wanted to BE. You will start to HAVE the life you always dreamt of by receiving all that comes your way because you are now BEING this person.

## BONUS—GOAL:

Now that you are a runner who is fit, perhaps a fun way to test your growth and newly developed skills is to create a GOAL—not just to finish a marathon but to finish it in a specific time!

Can you see how this second process might work for you more effectively? It's a whole different mental and physical vibe, connecting you to the energy and flow of it all on a whole different level.

## YOUR IDENTITY STATEMENT

When I work with clients one-on-one or in The Aligned & Empowered Project, the first step we take is to figure out their Identity Statement.

I personally also check in with my own Identity Statement throughout different seasons of my life.

Starting here, always coming back to here, is how you will lay a solid foundation from which you'll build the life of your dreams.

It's just like how businesses and organizations start with their mission and vision. This is your personal mission and vision statement.

If I'm working with a client for a long time, or if the ladies stay in The AEP grad program longer, we'll rework their statements depending on where they want their focus to be moving forward.

Once we identify their Identity Statement, I encourage them to print out a Declaration of Identity certificate that gives them space to declare who it is they are committed to being.

In fact, the certificate is meant to be written in the present tense, as if you already are that person.

It starts with "I am someone who_____" and then we date it ninety days in advance (I generally work with clients a minimum of ninety days or three months at a time).

Ideally, my clients check in with this statement, this affirmation, daily. Living into that person, connecting with that beingness as often as possible.

## EXAMPLE IDENTITY STATEMENTS

Your Identity Statement needs to connect with *you* and who *you* want to be, but I suggest you get as specific as possible.

Not so specific that you are stating the things you'll do to be that person, but rather be super clear about who it is you are trying to be.

Here some of my favorite examples of Declaration of Identity Statements from the ladies of The AEP:

## I AM SOMEONE WHO MAKES DECISIONS FOR ME, ABOUT ME, BECAUSE OF ME

Perfect for someone who is constantly saying *yes* to things because someone else told them they should. Also great for someone who struggles with self-worth.

## I AM SOMEONE WHO PRIORITIZES MY NEEDS ABOVE ALL ELSE

Great for the mommas out there who struggle with filling their cup first because society has told them that it isn't how good parents behave.

## I AM SOMEONE WHO CREATES KIND AND CLEAR BOUNDARIES UNAPOLOGETICALLY TO PROTECT MY ENERGY

Great for the person who is a people-pleaser and loses themselves to what everyone else needs. They often get burned out because they don't know how to say *no*. (We'll get into boundaries later in this book.)

· · ·

## I AM SOMEONE WHO IS UNAPOLOGETIC ABOUT GOING AFTER MY DREAMS AND GOALS

Great for that person who is looking to build a business or climb the ladder at work but feels like they need other people to agree with their ambitions or give them permission to do so. There have been one or two "mommaprenuers" in The AEP who have taken this Identity Statement on as their own.

## I AM SOMEONE WHO STANDS IN MY POWER AND REMINDS MYSELF WHO THE F I AM EVERY DAY

Great for the person who feels like they have lost themselves to all the circumstances of life (work, family, finances) and wants to get back to the powerful being they used to be.

## I AM SOMEONE WHO IS COURAGEOUS AND TAKE RISKS IN ORDER TO GET WHAT I DESIRE

Great for the person who lets fear dictate their every move. So many people allow the fear of failure to take the driver's seat and therefore miss out on opportunities. If you are someone who wants to make an impact in the world, *you* must *let your light shine*, and that includes doing things that make you uncomfortable.

. . .

There are plenty more statements where these came from, and if we work together, I'll help you customize one perfectly for you (or you can adjust one of the above to fit your needs).

The two most important elements in an Identity Statement are:

1. It must be a specific, clear, and stated in the affirmative.
2. I don't recommend using statements that include words like "don't" or "can't" or "without" or "anymore." For example, do *not* say, "I am someone who doesn't listen to other's negative feedback." A more powerful statement would be "I am someone who knows feedback is neutral and uses it to empower my future."
3. It must *feel good* to you.
4. If you don't connect with your Identity Statement, you aren't going to feel this process at your core. If you don't buy in here, at step one, then this isn't going to work for you. Lean in, let the ego take the back seat (more on this later), and work the program.

The Identity Statement is the first step in learning how to truly STAND IN YOUR POWER. This is the first step in finding alignment and allowing yourself to feel empowered to move forward on *your* terms.

Your Identity Statement should be easy to repeat, like an elevator pitch. If I was to ask you on any random day what your statement is, you should be able to say it back simply.

Because you know it.

Because it is your north star.

Because it is how you BE every day.

Because it is you.

This is your foundation.

This is and always will be your first step.

This is how we BE.

Next up we'll get to the fun stuff (at least for me): the *doing* of it all.


## DO THE DAMN THING

Time to take action and DO the first step of BEING.

Take some time to journal out who you want to BE at the end of ninety days (or this week, or this month, or this year). Use adjectives to describe how you will BE. Confident, curious, brave, bold, unapologetic, etc.

Head over to www.MaryTheresaTringale.com/book to grab a free Identity Statement training and download the Declaration of Identity Certificate to hang in your room, office mirror, bathroom, closet—wherever you will see it most. Keep it close and remind yourself daily *who* you desire to BE. This will help keep you going.

# TWO

# Habits—The "Doing"

"All big things come from small beginnings. The seed of every habit is a single, tiny decision. But as that decision is repeated, a habit sprouts and grows stronger. Roots entrench themselves and branches grow. The task of breaking a bad habit is like uprooting a powerful oak within us. And the task of building a good habit is like cultivating a delicate flower one day at a time."
—James Clear, *Atomic Habits*

## DECIDE THIS IS GOING TO WORK

THIS CHAPTER IS FOR ALL MY "DOERS" OUT THERE. IF THAT is you, you are welcome.

And also, I'm sorry.

I'm sorry because I'm not going to let you DO it all right this second. In fact, if you are anything like me, trying to do all the things all at once and then ultimately burning out and eventually doing nothing at all is likely how you got yourself here in the first place.

I see you. I hear you. This chapter is for you.

This chapter is also for all my "non-doers" in the house. Everyone who just plain-old doesn't want to do anything for whatever reason. Maybe for you, doing seems too hard, or maybe you get overwhelmed by the big picture (Ninety days of this? No way!), or maybe it seems impossible.

To you I say: Cool—you do you! But no action brings no results. So, choose right now: are you going to stay here forever or allow for something new? The choice is yours.

Nothing changes if nothing changes.

So, this chapter is also for you.

Finally, for all my people in between, who are great at getting started, maybe even incredibly good at not biting off more than you can chew and managing some sort of balance.

For those of you who have every intention of sticking it out this time, but, inevitably, life always seems to get in the way. Other things take priority, and before you know it, you are right back where you started.

This chapter is also for you.

Small, daily actions will lead to massive internal—and external—change.

There are some mantras I repeat to myself on the regular that I want to share with you:

**Everything you see on the outside is just a by-product of the work you're doing on the inside**.

**Focus on what you can control.**

**Get comfortable with the uncomfortable.**

**Everything you want in life is on the outside of your comfort zone.**

**Work the program. Work the process.**

**The Universe is not on your timeline, it's on the perfect timeline. Release the need for having it all right now. It will come when the time is right.**

These mantras may not make sense today, but they will become clear as you embark on this journey. It might be useful to write these down on some Post-Its and place them around the house as reminders.

Or, head over to www.MaryTheresaTringale.com/book to download these mantras and hang on your wall.

When I first started my own journey with habits while doing 75 Hard, I had been both the "do it all right now" person and the "do it all in a balanced way but life gets in the way" person.

I would burn out or find excuses to stop.

I never let the process truly work for me.

I had also done thirty-day diets that ended on day thirty-one, and I quickly gained all my weight back.

I had also lost my mind in the process trying to reach the finish line (again, never allowing myself to connect with my *why* or who I was desiring to be in the process).

I was terrified of putting myself out there to begin a journey of seventy-five days, one that so many people had been failing at left and right, and having it be yet another thing I didn't finish in my world.

But I was determined to turn my life around, and I knew this was the way to do it. It was free, and there was proof from others that it could work if I let it.

If. I. Let. It.

I realized that I hadn't ever really given any program the time, attention, and dedication it deserved to truly let it work its magic.

I was constantly giving up after ten days, twenty days, thirty days, because "nothing was happening."

But the truth was, I wasn't letting the process happen. I wasn't letting it work for me.

I was on a timeline that I created out of thin air, and that was that.

I wasn't ever allowing the process to happen for me. I was resisting because I had expectations, and those expectations weren't being met. Therefore, whatever I was doing "didn't work for me."

The shift and commitment that made it different for me this time around was deciding this 75 Hard journey was now my number 1 priority.

I committed to doing whatever I had to do to make it through to the end, from day one to day seventy-five, without failure.

Nothing would stop me.

Nothing.

I *had* to make this promise to myself. *I had to.*

I was riding along a consistent downward spiral, and if I kept letting the circumstances of my life get in the way, I was never going to find my way back up.

The hardest part of it all was that I was living in a world that was completely out of my control.

I realized what I had to do was *focus only on what I* could *control*, and let the rest just ride.

And,

I had to take it One. Day. At. A. Time.

Meaning, I wasn't going to keep track of how many days I had left. That was too daunting.

My focus was only on this day, and this hour, and this minute. I never let myself get ahead—never thought about how many days were left, because that didn't matter. What mattered was that one day, winning that one day.

In reality, I couldn't think further ahead even if I wanted to.

When it came to my dad, we never knew what the next moment would bring.

So, instead of allowing that reality to derail me, I leaned in found a way for it to work *for* me instead of *against* me.

As you know, I had certain habits/tasks I had to get done each day:

- Progress pic
- Follow a diet, no alcohol
- Gallon of water
- Workout two times a day for forty-five minutes, once outside

- Read ten pages a day of a self-improvement book

If I wanted to make these things happen, I had to control what I could control. Here are some of the things I could control:

- Making sure I took a progress pic each morning as soon as I woke up.
- Making sure I had a glass of water next to my bed to start drinking each day.
- Making sure I carried water around with me everywhere I went.
- Making sure I went to the bathroom before I did anything!
- Making sure there was always food in the house that aligned with my diet.
- Making sure I always had my walking shoes ready in case I had to cancel a workout and could only walk (which happened).
- Making sure I read first thing in the morning so that I didn't forget by the time I was too tired to stay awake and read.
- Making sure I communicated with my family what I needed in order to get my things done so that I could be available for them throughout the day.
- Making sure I was present when eating and drinking water so that I tracked it and didn't mess up.
- Making sure I was allowing myself time to reflect on the journey so that I could understand exactly what was happening.

- Making sure I got enough sleep so that I could wake up early and get my reading/workout done first thing and provide more time and space throughout the day.

When I started to focus on what I could control each day, the things I couldn't control became secondary. There was always something I could take responsibility for to set myself up for success, even during the most difficult days of my life.

I share my journey of 75 Hard with you because this chapter is about the small, daily habits that you can do consistently that will help make big changes in your life.

This is how you bring your "being" to life, with aligned action.

But first, you must commit and decide that you will do what it takes to win. That you *will work the program, every single day.*

If you only half commit or decide from the get-go that this process isn't going to work, then guess what …

You will be right.

So take it day by day, hour by hour, minute by minute, and be committed to making it happen *for* you.

## THE ROAD TO MASTERY

To really hammer home this point about sticking to your habits every day, I wanted to share a perspective from *Atomic Habits.*

In his book, Clear talks about how long-lasting growth comes not from going from zero one day to one hundred the next—that is not sustainable (which is another reason why so many people fail at maintaining habits).

For example, on one coaching call while discussing habits in The AEP, one of the ladies declared, "I am someone who is healthy" (not a great Identity Statement by the way, too broad). When I asked, "What does healthy look like?" she answered, "Going to the gym every day, eating well every day, managing my mental health, etc."

Whew—just writing that gave me *agita*.

If it seems like that is *a lot* to do every day, you would be right.

These are *very* tall orders and expectations to put on ourselves and a *very* common way of taking action.

This is a perfect example of the going from "zero to one hundred" method that doesn't work, creating a cycle of consistent self-sabotage, not the consistent growth and momentum we are working toward here.

The *real* way to approach change is to implement *small*, consistent, daily habits that help you improve even 1 percent each day over time.

As Clear mentions, "If you get one percent better each day for one year, you'll end up thirty-seven times better by the time you're done."

This is a significant increase in development!

Clear also shares:

"Habits are the compound interest of self-improvement over time."

I love the ice cube example that Clear uses in *Atomic Habits* to show the power of only 1 percent difference—similar to the power of 1 degree.

> Imagine you are sitting in a room with an ice cube. The room is 25 degrees Fahrenheit. The room slowly gets warmer, one degree at a time.
> At 26 degrees—nothing happens
> At 27 degrees—nothing happens
> At 28 degrees—nothing happens
> At 29 degrees—nothing happens
> At 30 degrees—nothing happens
> At 31 degrees—nothing happens
> At 32 degrees—FINALLY, ice starts to melt.
> Magic.
> "A one-degree shift, seemingly no different front the temperature increases before it, has unlocked a huge change."

Just today, here in Maine, it was pouring buckets of rain and freezing. I looked at the dashboard of my car and saw it was 34 degrees. Two degrees away from all this rain being snow.

I love this quote from *Atomic Habits* that really hits this point home for me: "Complaining about not achieving success despite working hard is like complaining about an ice cube not melting when you heated it from 25 to 31 degrees. All the action happens at 32 degrees."

What a difference it would have made not only for my mood, but for the entire day if all that rain had actually been snow.

It's the same with your habits. Small, consistent, daily action steps will deliver major changes and results, over time, if you let them.

## ALIGNED ACTION

In the last chapter, we talked about *being* and how you must understand your *why* above all else. Otherwise, you'll have no connection to the process or habits you are implementing, and you'll likely find yourself right back where you started.

The second step in the process is to identify habits that are *aligned* with your desired beingness (and be committed to doing those habits).

If you start doing habits that some other guru told you to do but have no foundation of *why* those habits mean anything to who you want to be, then they will become a checklist of things that don't matter instead of meaningful actions toward who you want to be.

When I first read *Atomic Habits*, I had already completed my first round of 75 Hard and experienced some BIG shifts and growth in my life.

When I did read the book, I was blown away. Everything Clear described about habits was exactly what I had experienced during 75 Hard.

Without realizing it, I had my *why*: I wanted to be someone who was disciplined and an athlete again.

This program provided me the habits and process that would allow to be both.

My *why* might be different from yours, and I definitely do not believe you have to do 75 Hard to see a big difference in your life.

But I do think you need to DO something—we all need to do something—in order to keep growing, evolving, BEING, and impacting the world.

And doing habits that align best with who *you* want to be is going to make a difference. I promise. This is why step one was BEING and now, in step two, we are DOING.

So, what habits are best for you? Well, it depends.

You want your habits to be aligned with *who you want to be.*

Without having a deep conversation about what habits would be best, I really can't tell you here what the exact habits are that you should be doing—that would be a disservice.

What I *can* do is give you some suggested habits and ideal guidelines, and you take what works best for you!

## 1. CHOOSE ONLY 1–3 ALIGNED HABITS, DEPENDING ON YOUR LIFE LOAD

Be realistic. How many new tasks do you think you could do consistently for thirty days? I've had clients who could realistically only commit to one new habit, but they committed to that one habit like they never committed before. By the end of the thirty days, they had learned they had capacity for more, so they added on.

## 2. START WITH THIRTY DAYS AT A TIME

In The AEP, we have a thirty-day tracker process (we have a printed paper tracker to visually support the journey). We make the commitment to stick with the habits for thirty days, and then we reevaluate. We answer questions like: How did things go? Are you ready for more? Is your Identity Statement still valid? Are the habits still aligned?

## 3. GET ACCOUNTABILITY

The number 1 reason why I was successful with 75 Hard was because I found a way to be accountable outside of myself. I didn't have an accountability coach or buddy at the time (I have two now), but I knew that if I didn't find a way to be held accountable, I was probably going to give up. I ended up sharing every single habit, every single day, on social media.

I had to move through a lot of fears to do it, but it ended up being incredibly powerful for me. Finding a way to hold yourself accountable to this process is *essential* for success. In The AEP, I hold everyone accountable with daily check-in posts where I ask them to share wins, struggles, and their overall experience of the journey. My suggestion is that you find someone who can help you stay accountable to the process you have committed to—you don't have to do it alone.

# SUGGESTED HABITS

The following are some suggested habits you could consider aligning with your Identity Statement. Choose what works best for you or create one that feels good. These are not the only habits that can help, but they are some of the most common habits I see supporting my clients time and again.

**HABIT:** Walking thirty to forty-five minutes a day, *no matter what* (This means gear up. There no such thing as bad weather, just bad clothing.)

**WHY:** I'm going to go ahead and declare that walking is the most underrated form of movement out there. It totally does not get the respect it deserves (in my humble opinion), and if you are not walking daily, you are missing out.

There are *so* many health benefits, both physical and mental, to walking. If you visit www.MaryTheresaTringale. com/book, I share many different resources that discuss the benefits.

I'll also include resources to the health benefits of being outside in nature. It's a natural healer, in more ways than one. Especially when you get out there on the not-so-perfect days.

When it comes to The Aligned & Empowered Project, walking is the first habit I insist the ladies begin with, regardless of their Identity Statement (I'm that confident it is a habit that will support who they want to be).

If you don't have a walking habit already, this is where I want *you* to begin too. If you can only fit in one new thing a day, this is the one I want you to start with.

Here are a few ways walking in nature changed things for me:

- Gave me space to think and listen to my intuition
- Gave me opportunity to practice boundaries with friends, family, and myself
- Allowed me to connect with nature in ways I never knew I needed
- Allowed me time to disconnect from work and my business
- Gave me the opportunity to explore new areas in my neighborhood and beyond

- Allowed a free and accessible habit anywhere I went in the world
- Gave me an exercise I can enjoy with anyone, anywhere
- Gave me the opportunity to use that time for whatever I may need in that moment: silence, motivation, learning, entertainment
- Gave me the opportunity to ask big questions on walks, and receive big answers that I wouldn't have had the time and space to listen for otherwise

## FAQs About Walking

**Q:** Does walking my dog count?

**A**: Depends! Is your dog coming on your walk, or are you going on your dog's walk? There is a difference.

**Q:** Can I listen to music or a podcast?

**A:** Yes! Use that time on your walk for what *you* need. Sometimes I wear my headphones and listen to nothing because I naturally am listening to everything in my head. Sometimes I need to listen to Lizzo and strut while walking to raise my vibe. Sometimes I need silence so I can ask big questions and hear the answers. What I do suggest is that you start your walk with an intention, and then allow whatever you need to come to you.

**Q:** Can I do fifteen minutes in the morning and fifteen minutes in the afternoon?

**A:** This isn't ideal. It would be better for you to carve a good chunk of time out of your day for you to walk so you can really have a significant amount of time in your day for you. But, if this is the only way you'll do it, then do it. Just make sure you are walking *on purpose*.

**Q:** Can I walk with someone?

**A:** Sure, but not every day. The point of the walk is for it to be *about* you, *for* you. If you are always only waiting for someone else to go with you, you are never allowing for that space and time to breathe, hear, listen, and be. If being alone on a walk makes you uncomfortable, good! Because as my earlier mantra states: *everything you want in life is on the outside of your comfort zone.*

**Q:** Why outside no matter what?

**A**: Because it's very easy to go for a walk on a beautiful day. It's harder to say yes to walking when it's shitty out. This takes discipline and commitment, and, again, doing things outside your comfort zone. Turns out, you can do hard things. Start with walking outside no matter what.

**HABIT:** Journaling

**WHY:** Oh, let me count the ways. Journaling has been the second most impactful tool in my toolbox. If walking gives me the space and time to ask questions and hear the answers, journaling is the tool that allows me to get it out of my head and onto paper so that I can make sense of it all.

Again, there is actual scientific research that discusses the benefits of journaling for mental health. If you visit www.MaryTheresaTringale.com/book, I have a plethora of journaling resources for you there.

Following are tips on how journaling has worked for me and the practices I put into place to help me get clarity both inside and out.

## BRAIN DUMP BEFORE BED

Sometimes I am *so* full of things in my head when I go to bed, I struggle to calm down my brain in order to sleep. One technique my friend Arielle taught me is a brain dump. Grab your journal and write everything that is inside your head for as long as necessary.

You aren't making a comprehensive list; you aren't trying to make sense of it all. You are simply dumping all the words in your brain onto the page, getting what is inside out.

In the morning, if it is helpful, you can reread what you wrote in case you do need to make a to-do list for the day.

Or sometimes your brain dump might be a rant about how something went during the day or maybe even a conversation you would like to have or re-have.

Allow this time to be an opportunity to get what is happing inside your brain out onto paper so it is no longer taking up important real estate inside.

## ASK, LISTEN, WRITE

This practice also allows me to get in tune with my intuition.

Here is how I do it step-by-step:

1. Grab your journal and a pen you love to write with (if you know, you know).
2. Sit in a comfortable position.
3. Grab some headphones with calming music. I like the Manifestation playlist on Spotify.
4. Close your eyes and take a deep breath in through the nose for five seconds, hold at the top for five

seconds, release through your mouth for five seconds. Do this for a full minute.

5. Connect with your intuition/guides/God/Universe, whoever or whatever. Thank them all for being here with you.

6. Open your eyes and write at the top of the page: *Thank you guides/Universe of the highest truth and compassion for showing me what I need to know today.*

7. Write freely, without judgement, whatever comes to mind. Whatever you hear, feel, or see. Don't worry about complete sentences or making sense, just let it roll. Write for five to ten minutes or longer, whatever you need.

8. Reread what you wrote and allow it to soak in.

## JOURNAL PROMPTS

Personally, I don't always do well with journal prompts. I do much better with allowing myself to write whatever comes up for me. But sometimes, I need a little help, so I'll start with a specific question I am trying to work through.

I'll take the exact same steps as above, but instead of asking "what do I need to know today?", I'll ask a specific question and then allow for the free writing.

Here are some journal prompts that could get you going. If none of these spark your interest, Google "journal prompts for (fill-in-the-blank)" and see what comes up for you.

- What is blocking me from taking this next step in my job?
- Why am I feeling uneasy when I experience this at home?

- Why does this person trigger me when we are together?
- What did I hear my parents say about money growing up?
- What did I see in my childhood about job security growing up?
- What am I afraid of with this decision I have to make?
- Why am I afraid of money?
- Why am I afraid of traveling?
- What does happiness look like for me?
- What does my dream life look like? Where am I living? What kind of a home do I have? What am I wearing? Who am I talking to? What am I doing for work?
- Wouldn't it be cool if …?

**HABIT:** Meditation

**WHY:** Again, there are so many articles about the scientifically proven benefits of meditation for your mental health. I have some resources for you at www.MaryTheresaTringale.com/book. What I'm going to speak to here is how meditation has supported me in my journey.

Meditation is a doer's *worst* nightmare! Or, at least it was for me.

Sitting still doing nothing for ten minutes!? What a waste of time. At least with walking, I'm moving my body. How could meditation actually be beneficial?

If you want a great description of what it's like to truly get into a meditative state that creates pure bliss and balance, you should read Michael Singer's *The Surrender Experiment*.

He describes meditation in such a way that you may not be able to help yourself but try.

Meditation, for me, has been another tool in my toolbox that allows me to feel grounded and connect with my inner wisdom. I believe each of us has everything we need for creating the life of our dreams already within us. We just need a little help bringing the knowledge from the depths of our subconscious to our conscious.

When I meditate, I'm taking another opportunity to slow down and just be. Be connected, be grounded, be in receiving mode.

It also is a practice in understanding that I am not my thoughts; my thoughts are like clouds that pass on by. I can just witness them—they don't own me in any way.

If you are still freaking out a little about sitting in silence for any amount of time, I have good news for you. Supportive meditation practices are incredibly accessible. There are free guided sessions on Spotify and YouTube, or you can invest in an app or membership program. The important thing to know is that you don't have to do it alone.

What changed the game for me was live meditations with my friend Bea. She is a magical, spiritual human, and meditating with her was a game changer. She taught me how, encouraged me to give myself grace, and preached that whatever the meditation was for me, it was perfect, so no judging!

Meditation is the ultimate grounding tool for me. If I'm not grounded, I am spinning. I must always take the time to ground myself in order to be my best self and to be able to serve others as my best self.

If meditation is a habit you would like to add to your habit routine, I highly recommend you try different apps, methods, audios, and videos until you find one that feels good to you.

And remember, meditation is more than a habit, it's a practice. It takes time and consistency to get good at it, and the practice never ends.

**HABIT:** Reading ten pages a day (of a self-improvement or self-help book)

**WHY:** I must admit, sometimes I hate walking through the aisles of a bookstore into the clearly labeled "self-help" section. I worry others will see me and judge. I start to experience feelings of shame, as if there is something wrong with me and now I need help to fix me.

I think these book sections would be better identified as "self-improvement," because there isn't anything wrong with you or me. We want to improve and keep our growth growing.

"Once you stop learning, you start dying."—Albert Einstein

I have to make reading a priority first thing in the morning, or it likely won't happen. It isn't a habit that I'll stop in the middle of my day to do. I have to do it first thing in the morning, before anyone or anything can mess up my day.

If you don't know what book to read first, get a recommendation from a friend or check out my book list at www.-MaryTheresaTringale.com/book.

Another tip: commit to finishing the book completely. I don't know about you, but I'm infamous for starting a book and not finishing it. This habit keeps me accountable to not only reading ten pages a day, but also finishing the book.

After walking and journaling, reading self-improvement books have been a total game changer for me, especially as I stepped into the coaching space. I've learned so much about myself, my clients, my family, my community, and beyond.

The power of a book is incredible, and if you allow it to take you wherever you are meant to go, it could change your life big time.

**HABIT:** Power List

**WHY:** This one is for my "doers" and the "non-doers."

Raise your hand if you feel like your to-do list never gets smaller.

Raise your hand if you feel like you are constantly "doing" but never really moving the needle one way or another.

I hear you. I see you. And, man, have I got a tool for you.

This habit will help you turn your to-do list into a power list that moves the needle and brings all the small yet essential tasks to the front of the line so that you can truly make a difference in your business, life, and world.

This process is meant to help you break down the projects that are taking up space on your to-do list into small, actionable tasks that will create momentum.

Whenever my clients say on a call, "My to-do list is overwhelming and I can't seem to make a dent in it, no matter how hard I try," I know exactly what the problem is.

It's because they aren't being realistic about how many to-dos have to get done to make the BIG to-do a reality.

For example, if you have "paint bedroom" on your to-do list and you keep getting frustrated because you can't seem to buckle down and make it happen, this is why:

"Paint bedroom" isn't a to-do, it's a *project*. It has *many* to-dos that need to get done before "paint bedroom" can actually be crossed off the list!

Creating a power list for that project will be a game changer. It is essentially playing a mind game, allowing yourself to have smaller wins along the way instead of postponing any wins until the end. This will help you feel satisfied and accomplished each day, allowing you to *feel good* throughout the process (more on *feeling good* later!)

Want to learn how I use Post-Its to create the ultimate power list and how to use it as a powerful habit each day? I have a free training for you over at MaryTheresaTringale.com/book. It's a goodie, so don't sleep on this!

## DO THE DAMN THING

Here is where you take action.

Choose one to three habits (walking should *definitely* be one) and start now.

Download the thirty-day tracker to support you at MaryTheresaTringale.com/book and start tracking.

Watch the quick training on how best to utilize this tracker and share with me via tagging me on social media (@mary.theresa.tringale). I'll cheer you on!

After thirty days of killing it, add on. If you don't get to thirty days of straight wins, no problem. Stick with the three you've got and keep going for another thirty days and see what happens.

## You got this!

THE FIRST TWO CHAPTERS OF THIS BOOK WERE ALL ABOUT how to BE and how to DO. The remainder of this book consists of a number of tools, practices, and resources for you to lean into and learn how to HAVE.

You might be thinking "How to have? I don't get it, I know how to have!"

But do you?

You might be surprised to know that receiving is something many of us struggle with. I know I do, especially when I am receiving things I didn't wish for or desire.

What I have learned is that results come in all different shapes and sizes and as gifts of opportunity to continue to grow.

Leaning into the practice of receiving every challenge, outcome, or experience as an opportunity for growth isn't always easy. In fact, sometimes it may present itself as the most challenging time in your life.

However, *the only way out is through*, and when you can lean in and allow, magic can happen.

These are the tools I use regularly to help me through.

These are the tools I teach and encourage in The Aligned & Empowered Project.

Take what supports you, leave what doesn't. Come back to these chapters whenever you may need them, whenever you feel called to.

Let's do this.

# THREE

# Mindset and It's Good to Feel Good

"If parents want to give their children a gift, the best thing they can do is to teach their children to love challenges, be intrigued by mistakes, enjoy effort, and keep on learning. That way, their children don't have to be slaves of praise. They will have a lifelong way to build and repair their own confidence."
—Carol Dweck, *Mindset*

## WHAT THE HECK IS MINDSET ANYWAY?

I ONLY STARTED TO HEAR THIS TERM WHEN I BEGAN MY journey in the entrepreneurial space. I started listening to podcasts and reading books, and time and again I would be brought back to this word *mindset*.

It was "essential," as the entrepreneurial experts preached, for us entrepreneurs and high-performers to work on our mindset to ensure it was unshakable and strong, as the journey ahead would test us again and again.

It wasn't until I joined a business course that I really started to understand how essential mindset work was, not only as I was building a business, but as I started to really work on the relationship I had with myself, my family, and my community.

I have always been an advocate for therapy. I'm currently in therapy and have been for many years. I think there is nothing better than having someone in your corner who gets paid to listen to you bitch (it's the best really, they can't say no!).

But mindset work was proving to be a whole different ball-game. It requires a level of deep knowledge and understanding of why I believe and think the way I do and the emotions attached to those belief systems. Ultimately, I am in control of how I let it all drive me as I create the life I want for myself.

As I started seeing the results of deep mindset work with Nick (my coach I mentioned in chapter one who I have been working with closely since March 2020), I was having major "Aha!" moments and shifts that truly changed the game for me.

I realized I wanted to create similar awareness and results for my clients, so I started to dig into the work more.

It's hard to explain what happens when you allow yourself to get vulnerable, open up, and create awareness around the bullshit stories you are holding on to that are ultimately holding you back.

If there is one thing I know to be true about transformation, it is that it isn't possible without awareness.

Awareness is what happens when you let someone else see you and allow yourself to be vulnerable and honest so you can cut through the clutter that is your own bullshit.

Mindset work can be challenging, especially for those of us who love to be *right* and *perfect* at all times (raise your hand if you feel me on this one; mine is as high as can be).

It is, however, essential for growth and evolution to allow ourselves to see another way, a better way, that we can live into and thrive from.

## FIXED MINDSET VERSUS GROWTH MINDSET

Understanding the difference between a fixed mindset versus a growth mindset has been another essential tool in my toolbox, playing a major role in my own journey toward being the person I desire to be.

I learned about fixed versus growth mindset from the book *Mindset: The New Psychology of Success* by Carol Dweck. This is an *incredible* book for parents, teachers, coaches, and basically all humans in general who want to evolve in life and help others do the same.

This is an important module to start with in The AEP because we refer back to it throughout the process as participants come against different mindset challenges and roadblocks that might knock them off their game.

As you enter into this new journey for yourself, I hope understanding fixed versus growth mindset helps you as much as it helped me.

## FIXED MINDSET

Your fixed mindset is what you were born with: your conditioning, limiting beliefs, and stories you have created around why things are the way they are.

A fixed mindset is just that—fixed. It is set in one place. Things "are the way they are," and that is all there is to it. In *Mindset*, Dr. Dweck describes fixed mindset as "believing that your qualities are carved in stone."

- Either you are talented, or you aren't
- Either you are smart, or you aren't
- Either you are charming, or you aren't
- Either you have the skills to create (fill-in-the-blank), or you don't
- Either you are successful, or you aren't

Dr. Dweck speaks to the fixed mindset being a hindrance to success rather than an asset.

Additionally, if you have done mindset work before, you may also know the fixed mindset as your limiting beliefs. These are the belief systems in your life that keep you small, hold you back from taking inspired action, and allow you to let fear take the lead.

However you would like to name it, (I'll be calling it "fixed mindset" from here on out) it's all a loud voice inside trying to keep you in one place, because that place is safe and known. Your fixed mindset is happy when you are safe and small, but that doesn't mean *you* are happy. This is why it's important to learn how to move away from the fixed mindset.

You are not your thoughts. You are just *experiencing* your thoughts. So, you get to teach your thoughts/mindset that there is another way.

## GROWTH MINDSET

The growth mindset implies that you can learn anything, that any skill can be developed, that failure is feedback for growth, and that talent and brains are developed over time.

Yes, some people might have to work harder at developing and learning skills than others, but it is possible to grow and develop into the person you desire to be.

Dr. Dweck says that the growth mindset is "believing that your basic qualities are things you can cultivate through your efforts, your strategies, and help from others."

## EMBRACE AND ACKNOWLEDGE THAT FIXED MINDSET

Think back to a time that you had something to say. Something you felt was important. You wanted to add to the conversation, and you felt you had something of value to add.

You raise your hand to be acknowledged and …

You are ignored …

Told to put your hand down …

Passed by …

Spoken over …

fill-in-the-blank.

How did that make you feel?

Small? Unworthy? Not capable? Not valued?

I hear you. I see you. I'm with you.

Then what happened?

Did you start to build resentment? Did you never raise your hand again but the things you needed to say built up inside? Did you get triggered one day and suddenly, you snapped, and everything you ever wanted to say came rushing out like the worst word vomit you could ever imagine?

Yeah. Again. I see you. I hear you. I'm with you.

This is essentially what happens when we try to ignore that fixed mindset.

What we resist, persists.

When we try to ignore the messages our fixed mindset is trying to tell us, we are resisting those messages. They won't go away because we are trying to ignore them, they are still there hiding in the dark, or under the rug, or in the closet.

## JOURNEY TO TRUE GROWTH MINDSET

So, if we aren't supposed to let the fixed mindset take the lead but also aren't supposed to ignore it, what *can* we do about it?

Have no fear, Dr. Dweck is here.

In *Mindset* Dr. Dweck shares the Journey to a True Growth Mindset. I'll share those steps with you here quickly, and you can dig in more when you read the book:

## 1. EMBRACE YOUR FIXED MINDSET

This is what I was referring to before. Don't ignore your fixed mindset but rather, embrace it.

Say, "Hey you, fixed mindset, I see you there. I hear you." Remember, what you resist persists, so if you resist the fixed mindset (aka, sweep it under the rug and don't give it space to breathe), then you are going to give it the fuel it needs to be persistent in showing up in your life again and again.

See it, embrace it, and give it a good old hug because it isn't going to be sticking around for long.

## 2. RECOGNIZE YOUR TRIGGERS

Again, awareness is the first step in any transformation. If you don't know what the heck the problem is, you can't fix it.

Taking the time to understand *what* triggered your fixed mindset popping up is essential for moving forward into the growth mindset. How do you do that?

Take the time to slow down—pause—and ask the question, "How did I get here? What just happened that made my fixed mindset come out of the woodwork?" (This is an *excellent* journal prompt, by the way!)

Maybe it was when a family member gave unsolicited advice about the way you wear your hair, or the friend who suggested your side hustle wouldn't work, or when you saw someone from your past at the grocery store and felt the urge to run in the other direction.

Whatever the trigger was, take note. It's important in order to move forward.

## 3. GIVE YOUR FIXED MINDSET PERSONA A NAME

Dr. Dweck encourages you to create a personality/name for your fixed mindset. I feel this helps to remind us that we are not our fixed mindset, we are just *experiencing* the thoughts and feeling of that persona.

Giving the fixed mindset a name allows you to take control, in a way, making it clear that it is separate from you, and you are going to work to keep it that way.

It's helpful to name the persona after someone who you don't particularly care for or relate to. In The AEP, the ladies choose the names of people from their past who didn't respect them or see them, or pick a nickname they were called that they didn't love.

This exercise is to remind you that as much as you are completely separate from another human, you are completely separate from your fixed mindset. And now you get to call it what it is—*not you*!

My fixed mindset is Matilda, a nickname I was called as a child because I wasn't particularly quiet and "ladylike" growing up. When I was being wild and sassy, I was called Matilda. Now, she has a new role in my life.

## 4. EDUCATE YOUR PERSONA—SHOW IT THERE IS ANOTHER WAY

Take your fixed mindset on the journey with you and educate it by taking action and showing it how things can be different.

Remember, nothing changes if nothing changes. This is your chance to show your fixed mindset what will *actually* happen if you try (versus the stories you have made up in your head about what *might* happen if you try).

The script I like to have in my head is this (and feel free to copy and paste for yourself): "Okay, Matilda. I see you coming here and telling me that I need to hush up and calm down because it isn't ladylike to do what I'm doing. I see you trying to keep me safe. But I'm going to give my voice and power a chance to try anyway. Let's see what happens together."

By doing this, I'm providing opportunity for Matilda to have a new experience, build a new perspective about how things can be.

As you practice this method more and more, eventually the voices will quiet down, because they have learned that fixed way of thinking doesn't have a hold on you anymore like it used to.

Let me be clear: doing this process doesn't promise Matilda will go away forever. Unfortunately, Matilda is like a damn onion: so many freaking layers. Once you peel one away, there is another one right underneath.

The good news is that once you master this process, it will become second nature, and you'll be able to move through the BS faster than you ever have before!

## IT'S GOOD TO FEEL GOOD

Raise your hand if you have ever felt guilty about feeling good.

Raise your hand if you have ever felt guilty about prioritizing yourself over others in order to feel good.

Raise your hand if you are Italian and you heard growing up, "Don't let yourself feel too happy, the other shoe is going to drop soon."

Raise your hand if you are Irish and you were told from a young age, "Don't get too full of yourself, there is always someone suffering more than you. You should be giving your joy to them because they need it more than you do." Or something like that?

Yeah, I see you. I hear you. I'm with you.

And also, I'm here to tell you: It's good to feel good!

Like, *really* good to feel good.

When you feel good, the world benefits.

When you feel good, you create a ripple effect of change for your community.

When you feel good, you communicate with love, take aligned action, and have space to support others when they need you (like all the suffering people of the world).

This is when I tell you that your absolute number 1 priority in life is to *fill your cup first*. Put on your oxygen mask first. Go for your walk first!

You cannot be the best mom, sister, cousin, niece, granddaughter, employee, or employer if you are not taking care of yourself first, if you are not prioritizing feeling good above all else.

This isn't to say it isn't okay to feel bad. It's the opposite really.

This is to say that being in touch with your emotions and feelings, understanding them, seeing them, giving them space to breathe, and then doing the work you need to do to raise your vibe should be your priority. (This is step one in the journey to a growth mindset).

How? Well, glad you asked.

Another one of my favorite tools in my toolbox that I teach in The Aligned & Empowered Project is author Gabby Bernstein's Choose Again Method found in her book *Super Attractor*.

In *Super Attractor*, Bernstein talks about how we aren't supposed to go from experiencing sadness or depression one minute and immediately find ourselves in joy the next.

In fact, having that expectation for ourselves is not only unrealistic but also harmful.

Raise your hand if you have ever been frustrated with yourself because you weren't able to push those feelings of sadness or depression aside and instantly get to happiness or joy like you desired.

Guess what, you are 100 percent human, congrats!

Bernstein talks about how we have to be able to move our way through the Emotional Scale (this is also talked about in *Ask and It Is Given* by Esther and Jerry Hicks; read this to learn all about the collective known as Abraham and all you really need to know about the Law of Attraction) in order to allow ourselves authentic emotional change.

Moving your way through the emotional scale is essential for getting into a true high-vibrational state so that you can attract high-vibe experiences, things, and people into your life. Here is the Emotional Scale according to Abraham-Hicks:

## THE EMOTIONAL SCALE

1. Joy/Appreciation/Empowered/Freedom/Love
2. Passion
3. Enthusiasm/Eagerness/Happiness
4. Positive Expectation/Belief
5. Optimism
6. Hopefulness
7. Contentment
8. Boredom
9. Pessimism
10. Frustration/Irritation/Impatience
11. Overwhelment (feeling overwhelmed)
12. Disappointment
13. Doubt
14. Worry
15. Blame
16. Discouragement
17. Anger
18. Revenge
19. Hatred/Rage
20. Jealousy
21. Insecurity/Guilt/Unworthiness
22. Fear/Grief/Desperation/Despair/Powerlessness

The best way to think about this is that in order to get from fear to joy, you have to allow yourself the opportunity to feel the emotions twenty-one through two. If you are trying to jump into joy without doing the work, you'll get really, really frustrated because it won't work, and you'll quickly find yourself right back where you started.

So, what can we DO to HAVE the high vibes and all the things that come along with it?

## THE CHOOSE AGAIN METHOD

This is a method I do on the regular, especially on the days I'm experiencing frustration or sadness or anger and I want to be in a higher-vibe state. I suggest you start this practice in your journal. Eventually you should be able to just do it on the fly, wherever and whenever you may need it.

## 1. NOTICE THE THOUGHT

*Any time you're stuck in negativity or fear, take a step back by consciously noticing that your thoughts and energy are out of alignment with joy. Ask yourself, "How do I feel right now?" You can write down your answer in your journal.*

**M-T NOTE:** In *Super Attractor* Bernstein encourages you to also mention the trigger (sound familiar?)

In your journal, write: "When ____happens, I feel _____"
An example may be, "When I don't reach my target revenue numbers, I feel frustrated and disappointed."

## 2. FORGIVE THE THOUGHT

*Forgive yourself for being misaligned and celebrate your desire to shift. Thank your negative feelings and thoughts for showing you what you don't want and revealing what you do.*

*Say this prayer: "Thank you (feeling/emotion/thought) for revealing to me what I don't want so that I can clarify what I do want."*

**M-T NOTE:** This step, in my experience, is where many go wrong or miss the opportunity. Also, it is the *most* important step.

Why?

Because in this step, you are not only forgiving the thought/emotion for existing, you are also giving yourself grace for having the thought in the first place, at the same time.

It isn't helpful to be hard on yourself because you aren't thinking perfectly 100 percent of the time.

**NEWSFLASH**—no one thinks perfectly 100 percent of the time. You are human. You are flawed. It's just the way it is.

Also:

You get to have tools in your toolbox that help you do better. This is one of them.

### 3. CHOOSE AGAIN

*Answer this question in your journal: "What is the best-feeling thought I can find right now?" Then ask the Universe to guide you toward that thought.*

*In your journal, write down this prayer or say it to yourself: "Thank you, Universe, for guiding my thoughts toward good-feeling emotions."*

**M-T NOTE:** This step may be tricky at first, especially if you aren't super in-tune with your inner wisdom.

A great trick is to think of a positive memory that brings you joy; that memory will help raise your vibe.

I do encourage you to take time and practice listening to the inner wisdom the Universe provides to you.

When I'm asking the Universe for guidance, I like to take a few moments to meditate with some deep breathing to get grounded and into the right mental space to receive the information.

I'll say the prayer above and wait and listen. The guidance might come in a happy memory, a new idea, or a new thought that reminds me of a better way of feeling.

## HAVE IT ALL BY BEING IN TUNE

My message to you in this chapter is that in order to start HAVING the life of your dreams, the one you are BEING and DOING in order to receive, you have to have a solid grasp of your mindset, and you have to be in constant pursuit of *feeling good*.

It's a simple way of looking at it, but it isn't easy. And that's okay. Hard isn't always bad. Hard can also feel good sometimes.

Let's keep going.

**DO THE DAMN THING**

Grab your journal—it is time to take action:

1. Name that fixed mindset! Go through the entire process of moving to the growth mindset, name that persona, and start referring to that fixed mindset as the persona. Get into the habit of knowing that you are *not* your fixed mindset—it is separate from who you are in your soul. **BONUS:** Once you name your fixed mindset, share with me on social media, and I'll cheer you on as you work to teach it new ways of being!

2. Work the Choose Again Method next time you are not feeling 100 percent. Allow yourself to move through this process and then do it again and again until you are at the top of the

emotional scale. Lean on this method, go back to it, let it be one of the most consistent tools in your toolbox that you reach for when you are experiencing a feeling or emotion you would rather not be experiencing.

# FOUR

# Agreements, Stories, and Awareness

"A belief is just a thought you keep thinking. When you choose a new thought, a shift will occur."
—Gabrielle Bernstein, *Super Attractor*

## THE POWER OF AGREEMENTS

THINK BACK TO WHEN YOU WERE A KID HAVING INTENSE discussions on the playground about *really* important topics, like which is the better TV show: *Saved by the Bell* or *Full House*? (For those of you reading who don't know these shows, YouTube them. Classics, I tell you—classics.)

Do you remember having such a strong opinion about whatever topic you were discussing to the point that maybe you got in a fight with a friend and maybe, possibly, it "ended" the friendship on the playground for the rest of recess?

Did you ever have someone ask you, "How do you know that?" and the only thing you knew to say was, "My Mom/Dad told me so"?

Yeah, me too.

This, my friend, is where I share with you what AGREE-MENTS are.

I was first introduced to agreements in the book *The Four Agreements* by Don Miguel Ruiz. I loved this book not only because of the four actual agreements he discusses but also because of the concept of what an agreement is in the first place.

In summary (read the book if you want to dive in deeper) an agreement is, according to Miguel Ruiz, something that our society has "domesticated us" with by creating "rules" about the world that we have agreed to.

For example, the thing above us is called the "sky," and the color it often is on a clear day is "blue."

These are agreements we have made. Someone long, long ago decided to call the thing above us "sky" and decided the color it would be called was "blue," and we all agreed to it. We just said "Yup, that's what it is!" and it is fact.

But truly, we could decide one day, if we wanted to, that the sky is, in fact, not blue but actually purple. We could plain-old decide that the sky's color is now called "purple," and there is nothing you can do about it.

Basically, if we look at all the agreements we live by day to day, we could technically decide, nope, I now agree to something else.

This is *not* me advocating that we should all decide to break the law and decide a new way of living. I don't want to create chaos in the world, but I do want to use this tool as a way to check in on our belief systems and stories we hold to be true in our own lives.

Think about the places in your life where you have adopted some agreements that possibly are holding you back from having the life of your dreams.

Here are a few example agreements I have had (either past or present) that are not very supportive in helping me reach my goals:

**AGREEMENT:** I am someone who has no choice but to hustle and grind for success.

**AGREEMENT:** I don't have what it takes to break through and become someone who matters.

**AGREEMENT:** I am not lucky enough to land a high-paying client or job like other people.

Can you see how these agreements can hinder my success more than help? If these are the beliefs I have, of course I'm not going to be this big successful entrepreneur I dream of being, right?

Okay, let's move on to STORIES. We'll come back to these agreements in a bit.

## WELL, THAT'S A NICE STORY

Our limiting beliefs aren't merely simple agreements. If they were, they would likely be easy to adjust because there wouldn't be any emotional charge attached to them.

For example, we don't really have any emotional baggage attached to "the sky is blue," right? If someone started calling it something else, it would be confusing, but you would probably be okay switching it up if necessary.

When we add a narrative to our agreements, we create an emotional attachment, anchoring in the agreement to truth, and we become connected to the story around the agreement as if it was the truth, the whole truth, and nothing but the truth, so help me God.

The narrative gives the agreement *life* and *meaning* and *connection* to who we are, why we are, and where we are.

Here are some examples attached to the agreements I mentioned before:

**AGREEMENT:** I am someone who has no choice but to hustle and grind for success.
**STORY:** This is a generational thing. My dad had to bust his ass, his dad had to bust his ass, and his dad before him. We are a family of hustlers; it's the only way to make ends meet. Nothing comes easily and without effort. You want to live a nice life? You better earn it, because we don't get things handed to us.

**AGREEMENT:** I don't have what it takes to break through and become someone who matters.
**STORY:** In order to be able to break through to the other side, I must have the right connections, the right support, and the right amount of money in order to get into the right rooms. I'll never have the resources or support needed to make it "big" in this world.

**AGREEMENT:** I am not lucky enough to land a high-paying client or job like other people.
**STORY:** Ever since I was little, I have watched everyone else around me get the "lucky break" and surpass me in everything that I did. Whether it was being invited to the high-level swim team, being able to get the designer jacket of the year, or being asked to play a leadership role at work when I worked just as hard, I have consistently been passed

over for others because I'm just not lucky enough to have what it takes to be worthy of the success.

Can you see how when I create narratives around my agreements, they become believable? You might even agree with these statements without actually knowing me because I've created quite the reasonable story around why each one is true.

What helps me with these narratives is that I have proof that they are true. Proof from my past experiences or my family's past experiences.

Proof, by the way, is also the thing that feeds Matilda to do her *thang* when the time is right …

It's an endless cycle of agreement, narrative, proof, agreement, narrative, proof. On and on and on.

Do you see this cycle of self-sabotage?

Reminder, I'm teaching you about agreements and stories because I want to help you HAVE the life of your dreams.

I realize up to this point I've only been talking about the negative sides of agreements and stories, but I promise you, there is a point to all of this, and I'm going to teach you how to end the cycle of self-sabotage so you can STAND IN YOUR POWER!

Ready?

## REWRITE YOUR STORIES SO THEY WORK *FOR* YOU INSTEAD OF *AGAINST* YOU

The best news about agreements and stories is that you can create *new* agreements and *new* stories any time, any place.

Just as I can decide one day that you will no longer be calling the color of the sky "blue," I can just as easily decide that I am lucky enough to receive the highest-paying clients and job out there, and you can too!

What is hard about this process is that oftentimes you have to create the new stories and agreements for your life without proof that they are true.

Self-sabotage can come into play when you are trying to rewrite agreements based only on the proof you have already experienced. Rewriting stories based on old facts keeps you exactly in the same place.

Nothing changes if nothing changes.

Maybe this is your opportunity to have a new agreement around what proof is in the first place.

In *Think and Grow Rich*, Napoleon Hill says, "Whatever your mind can conceive and believe, it can achieve."

For me, my proof is my vision. Not just any vision, the vision I have for my future.

My vision is mine on purpose; it wasn't your vision, or someone else's, but *mine*. I get to use my vision as my proof that whatever I desire and believe to be true is exactly that —true.

From there, I rewrite and agree to new ways of believing and receiving.

I invite you to consider your vision and your desires as all the proof you need to believe.

As you lean into your vision and desires, it's time to rewrite your agreements and stories to work *for* you instead of *against* you so that the visions and agreements can become your reality.

## AWARENESS IS KEY

"But wait, how do I rewrite stories and agreements if I don't even know what stories and agreements I have?"

*Great* question, and you are right. You can't rewrite what you don't even know you are subscribed to. So let's take a beat and head back to the very beginning.

As mentioned before, *awareness* is the first step in transformation.

Therefore, you not only have to have awareness around the agreements and stories currently running your life, you also must have awareness around the vision you have for your future.

If you are stuck on figuring out what your stories, agreements, vision, and desire are, guess what: you are in luck. You already have the tools needed to get to the bottom of it all:

## WALKING, JOURNALING, AND MEDITATION

Yes, that's right. Your habits that you are hopefully already doing are going to help you BIG TIME to build awareness around the limiting beliefs holding you back. Here are some strategies to consider next time you "do" your habits:

**WALKING:** Go for a walk without music and listen to your thoughts. Ask yourself a question that supports your struggle. Maybe something like, "What is a story I have around success that isn't serving me?" and listen for the answer. See what comes up for you.

**JOURNALING:** This is a great place for you to either use a journal prompt like the question I have above for walking or to ask for guidance and free write. Maybe start with "Thank you, guides of the highest good and compassion, for revealing to me the stories that are not serving me and holding me back from my greatness."

**MEDITATION:** Spending some time in meditation, silent time, to hear the thoughts passing through your mind. Slowing down and listening for ten to twenty minutes will allow you to see the thoughts stopping you. It's great to start meditation with an intention. For you, perhaps your intention could be "to slow down and listen for the limiting beliefs keeping me in the same place time and again" and see what comes up.

## NEW STORIES, NEW RESULTS

In *Secrets of a Millionaire Mind* by T. Harv Eker (awesome freaking book for money mindset!) he describes the mindset process as this:

**Your programming creates your thoughts > your thoughts create your feelings > your feelings create your actions > your actions create your results.**

So, in theory: if you can change your programming, you can change your results.

Nothing changes if nothing changes.

Your programming is your limiting beliefs, agreements, or stories that often don't belong to you. Sometimes, they don't even belong to the person who passed them along to you.

Remember, we started this chapter talking about how agreements are often passed along generation to generation.

You get to be the one who breaks the cycle and creates new agreements and stories for future generations to come—*that* is how you STAND IN YOUR POWER.

The following are the steps I take to rewrite my own agreements and stories to work *for* me instead of *against* me. I'll use one of my previously shared agreements as an example.

## STEPS FOR REWRITING THE STORIES TO WORK FOR YOU

### 1. Identify the vision or desire you want to be true:

**a.** I desire working with millionaires and billionaires and helping them elevate their lives to make massive impact in the world.

### 2. Identify the limiting belief/story/agreement holding you have around this vision or desire:

**a. AGREEMENT:** I am not lucky enough to land a high-paying client or job like other people.

**b. STORY:** Ever since I was little, I have watched everyone else around me get the "lucky break" and surpass me in everything that I did. Whether it was being invited to the high-level swim team, being able to get the designer jacket of the year, or being asked to play a leadership role at work when I worked just as hard, I have consistently been passed over for others because I'm not lucky enough to have what it takes to be worthy of the success.

## 3. Write out the opposite agreement:

**a. NEW AGREEMENT:** I am the luckiest of them all and always in the right place, at the right time, ready to receive the good fortune of high-paying clients and high-paying jobs.

## 4. Create a new story to support the new agreement:

**a. NEW STORY:** Everywhere I turn, I receive opportunity. I walk by people on the street every day who could offer me the chance to support them as their employee or coach. The content I share on social media is always received by the perfect people, and I know that when my future clients are ready, they will find me and we will be a perfect match. I'm so lucky to be able to live in a day and age where reaching people around the world is easy and accessible and free. I am always connected to the exact people I need to be connected to in order to enroll the perfect client and sign on to a high-paying job.

Whew, I feel *powerful* just writing that out here! Can you feel the energy behind that new story, the empowerment to take control and ownership of my circumstances, the *belief* that it is going to happen for me, that it already *is* happening for me?

You can do this too! Rewriting our belief systems is a great practice for journaling and daily habits.

**NOTE:** If you are struggling to see your stories even after all this work, it might be beneficial to work with a coach or therapist to help bring them to the surface. I find that having someone else be a mirror for me is incredibly helpful as sometimes I am my own biggest block to seeing what I need to see.

## DO THE DAMN THING

As I mentioned, the first step in any transformation is *awareness*, and the best way that I know how to help you build awareness is to have you journal on it.

Head over to www.MaryTheresaTringale.com/book to grab some journal prompts that should help get you started. Don't forget to tag me in any "Aha!" moments you might have that you share on your social platforms!

# FIVE

# Boundaries and Communication

"Daring to set boundaries is about having the courage to love ourselves even when we risk disappointing others."
—Brené Brown
"You are responsible for what you say and do. You are not responsible for whether or not people freak out about it."
—Jen Sincero, *You Are A Badass*

## BOUNDARIES: HOW YOU PROTECT YOUR ENERGY

SINCE GOING THROUGH MY OWN PERSONAL transformation where I had to communicate boundaries with my family in a loving but effective way, even on the days my dad was passing, I have become incredibly passionate about boundaries and why we all need them in our lives.

Boundaries are a funny thing. If other people don't know how to have boundaries or haven't experienced other people having them, they might feel put off by others enacting them.

For example, I was with an old friend a few weekends ago. We are really great friends today, but in our past, we had our differences. As she was referring to the good old days, she was commenting on ways I used to be (with love, of course).

As I was thinking about the things we used to fight about when we were younger, I realized it was usually because I was holding boundaries that she didn't like. Because the boundaries I was putting in place to protect my energy didn't align with her and her needs, it turned our relationship (at the time) toxic.

No wonder people don't like putting up boundaries. It's hard to keep them, especially when the only example you have is when they turn a relationship toxic.

Boundaries are, however, necessary in order for you to protect your mental health (and physical heath) and regulate your nervous system.

They can also be the exact thing that *keeps* your relationship from turning toxic.

I know that when my boundaries are not being respected, I will get triggered beyond belief and start reacting instead of responding, which nine times out of ten doesn't end well for either party involved.

As I mentioned, boundaries can be hard to implement if you have never had anyone in your life exercise them before.

For example, if you find it hard to implement boundaries with your parents, it may be because your parents didn't have healthy boundaries with their parents.

Because of this, you have no example of how to set them in your own parent/child relationship, which can lead to frustration, anger, and reactions that aren't helpful for the relationship.

Another example may be in the workplace. Perhaps when you started your career, you had bosses and mentors who didn't have boundaries with colleagues, so you never learned what healthy workplace boundaries look like. And now you feel stuck working around the clock because you don't feel safe implementing boundaries with colleagues.

The good news is it is never too late to start learning how to incorporate boundaries into your life. It isn't always easy, and sometimes it is downright terrifying, but when you do start practicing them, they can be game changers.

## MY JOURNEY WITH BOUNDARIES

Before I share tips and tricks for implementing boundaries, I want to give a little insight to my journey to discovering the power of boundaries and how I implemented them into my life.

As I mentioned, I was someone who always had boundaries, but I can't say that I always put them in place in a loving and communicative way.

The first note I'll give is that boundaries without communication is ultimately setting you up for failure.

If you don't clearly state your needs with the person you are setting boundaries with, there is no possible way that they can respect your boundaries and give you the space you need.

Brené Brown said, "Kind is clear, and clear is kind."

The clearer you are about your boundaries, the kinder you are being to the other person involved.

When I first started 75 Hard, I was absolutely determined to not let anything stand in the way of getting all the things I had to get done, done.

For the first couple of days, this was no problem. I lived alone and had no one to answer to except myself. I was able to get my habits done without issue.

It got challenging when I had to go home and help with my dad. Suddenly, I had to tell my mom where I was off to twice a day and how I couldn't just eat anything she put in front of me.

For my parents, this new way of being was out of the ordinary.

Why was I going for walks two times a day? Why was I getting up at 5 a.m. to read? Why was I needing to pee every hour? Why was I even drinking so much water?

I realized quickly that in order for me to keep harmony between my family and me, I had to be clear about what I needed in order to support them in return.

Would it have been easier if my family let me do my thing without question? Sure, but that wasn't their M.O.

Old me, before I was having all this clarity and alignment from my walks, would have easily gotten frustrated from the questions and judgement from others.

But I was in 75 Hard-or-bust mode, and nothing would slow me down, including worrying about what my family would think about my new regimen.

So, I had to communicate. I kept it *kind* and *clear* and didn't leave room for negotiation.

I told my family I was doing a challenge (something I didn't really want to share, but knew I needed to in order to clearly communicate my needs), and this is what it consisted of (I listed out the tasks). I made it clear that I was happy to help in any way, but I needed the space and time to take care of me.

Each day, I planned ahead with my mother so I could go for walks and still give her the space and time she needed to do what she needed to take care of herself.

Eventually, my need for my time became the norm. No one questioned it. To this day, my mom expects me to go on one to two walks while I'm visiting and even questions the days I don't do it.

I kept up these habits even on the days my dad was actively passing away. Those were the days I needed them most. Again, communication was *key* for making it through.

My two brothers and I had to work together to make sure we were there for our parents. Being clear about our needs and being respectful of each other's boundaries was essential for us to get through that time together.

I share this with you because if you are feeling that boundaries are hard and impossible to implement with your family in challenging times, I encourage you to consider rewriting that story into something new that would work for you.

I admit, I'm lucky to have a family that mostly respects my boundaries and crazy challenges I take on. I understand not everyone is so lucky.

## IMPLEMENTING BOUNDARIES: 101

This is where I remind you that practicing boundaries isn't always easy. If it was, everyone would be doing it.

It is, however, a magical tool that will change your life for the better, if you let it.

When you use boundaries, your communication gets clearer and more effective.

When you use boundaries, your confidence begins to grow.

When you use boundaries, your energy is protected, and you may have more space to see triggers headed your way (so you can hold off the fixed mindset from taking control when you would prefer they kept to themselves).

Boundaries are opportunities for you to set others up for success.

Boundaries are a way for you to manage your own expectations and the expectations of others.

## TIPS FOR SETTING BOUNDARIES

### START SMALL

This is great if you are stepping into the world of boundaries and are feeling a lot of emotions around setting them with people in your life.

In The Aligned & Empowered Project we create non-negotiables with our daily habits. This means, they get done *no matter what*, which generally means setting boundaries either with yourself or the people who live in your space twenty-four hours a day (spouse, children, significant other, roommates, coworkers, etc.).

Starting like I did by setting boundaries with something that doesn't have too much emotion attached to it, like your habits, is a much less intimidating conversation to have than, say, having to talk about how you need more "alone time" in life with your significant other.

## START WITH YOU

The thing about boundaries is that they aren't only for protecting your energy from other people. You might need to start by setting boundaries with yourself first.

As we all know by now, sometimes the biggest obstacle standing in our way of success is ourselves. And one way to work through that is to set boundaries that keep us in-check with ourselves.

A few of the personal boundaries I have with myself are:

- Only two episodes of *Schitt's Creek* a night, then bed
- No screens in bed
- No meetings or calls scheduled to start after 7:30 p.m.

## "NO" IS A COMPLETE SENTENCE

Dr. Nicole Lepera, The Holistic Psychologist, is a great resource for all things boundary-related, including under-standing how "no" is a complete sentence.

She states: "Understand people's feelings are not your responsibility. How people feel about your actions is based on their own previous experiences in the world. They have little or nothing to do with you. You are not responsible for the feelings created from them."

So how do we do this? How do we say no and then step away? Well, by doing exactly that.

Too often we are afraid of setting boundaries because we are afraid of how the other person will react—and generally, they will (hell, we'll react when setting boundaries with ourselves!).

So, you need to be prepared to say no and then do what you have to do to block out their reaction. This might be walking away, leaving the house, shutting off the phone, blocking their DMs or emails, *whatever*—boundaries don't work if you allow space for negotiation.

Dr. Lepera also says to "let words be second to action: We as humans are used to communicating with each other via words, but with boundaries, you have to follow up with action (like shutting off the phone, walking away, blocking them, or doing what you say you are going to do if they break the boundary)."

This is especially important if you aren't used to setting boundaries. You have to be committed to doing the "new" thing (setting the boundary) and also following through with it. You have to commit to it like never before, and that sometimes means with a non-verbal action.

There is *so* much more to be said about boundaries, but if you take away one thing from this chapter, I hope it is this:

Boundaries are a necessity if you truly want to STEP INTO YOUR FULL POWER.

Without boundaries, you'll always be second to everything and everyone else in your life who demands your attention.

No one else is going to decide for you that you are number 1—*you* have to do it.

But once you do and you start implementing boundaries in your life, everyone in your life will benefit.

Everyone.

(For more on boundaries follow Dr. Lepera on Instagram @the.holistic.psychologist)

## DO THE DAMN THING

Here are some more journal prompts to help you kickstart your boundaries journey. Don't forget to share your "Aha!" moments with me on social media. Download these prompts and more at MaryTheresaTringale.com/book

- Who in my life can I set some healthy, loving boundaries with today so it will not only help me protect my energy, but it will benefit them too?
- Was I *kind* and *clear* in the direction I provided today? Could I have done better? If not, how can I communicate with (my spouse, my child, my boss) in a *clearer, more specific* way to create the kindest experience for all possible?
- What one boundary can I set with myself for the next seven days that if I stick with it, I'll be protecting my energy in the best way possible?

# SIX

# Accountability

"Accountability breeds responsibility."
—Steven Covey

"Asking for help isn't a sign of weakness, it's a sign of strength. It shows you have the courage to admit when you don't know something, and to learn something new."
—Barack Obama

"Be strong enough to stand alone, smart enough to know when you need help, and brave enough to ask for it."
—Ziad K. Abdelnour

## ACCOUNTABILITY IS QUEEN

WIKIPEDIA SAYS, "'IF A TREE FALLS IN A FOREST AND NO one is around to hear it, does it make a sound?' is a philosophical thought experiment that raises questions regarding observation and perception."

So let's try another one on for size:

"If you do habits throughout the day but don't have anyone to share your progress with, does it really matter"?

You might say, "Yes, of course," and I say, "Sure, but I'm probably not going to do them."

Anyone else with me on that one? I thought so.

When I first contemplated doing 75 Hard way back in June of 2019, there was one thing that was a sticking point for me—I wasn't confident I wouldn't give up on myself before the seventy-five days were up.

Years before, I was very good at being disciplined when it came to commitments I had made, like training for multiple Olympic distance triathlons or executing massive events by myself.

I know for a fact the number 1 reason I was successful in staying disciplined was because there were other people holding me accountable to whatever I had going on.

- I had managers and colleagues at work who held me accountable to getting my job done.
- I had friends and family who held me accountable to sticking to my word when I made a promise.
- I had coaches and fellow athletes holding me accountable to showing up to practice when I was training.

Someone was always watching, which was my driver for always showing up.

In spring of 2019, things looked very different.

I had gotten myself into a hole where I wasn't showing up for things (like going to the gym or being present on social media to promote my business). And because I wasn't showing up for others, no one was showing up for me in return.

It was exactly like the tree in the forest scenario: If I made a random commitment to a challenge that affected no one else but me and I never talked about it or mentioned it to a single soul, did it really happen?

I decided what I had to do in order to make it through the entire seventy-five days without failure was to find somewhere to hold myself accountable publicly. I decided this looked like sharing my entire journey, every single day, on social media.

I didn't know if people would watch me, or care, or get annoyed, but I knew that this was how I was going to keep my word to myself, and essentially to my community as a whole.

This was how I was going to be sure the falling of the tree was heard by all.

Yes, sharing *everything* on social media did scare the crap out of me. But failing this program that I committed to scared me more, so I had to do what I had to do to make sure I kept my word.

The sharing of my entire 75 Hard journey and beyond was probably the most magical decision I could have ever made for myself. It was how I unapologetically stepped into my power and created a ripple effect that is still going strong today.

When I shared my journey, I essentially did two things:

- Gave others permission to do the same
- Allowed others to show up for me in ways I never thought they would

When I allowed my community to be my accountability buddy, they showed up to cheer me on in droves. I had friends who I hadn't spoken to in years reach out in support, others ask for advice (which was the spark I needed to consider pivoting to accountability coaching), and neighbors stopping me on the streets of Portland to show support and encourage me to keep going.

As I have stepped into this space of being an accountability coach, I've heard from many who try to shame those of us who need help outside of ourselves to become the best version of ourselves.

If you have someone in your life who thinks that way, I suggest you create some serious boundaries with them immediately, and then I encourage you to consider this:

Our entire lives growing up, we get to have the support of someone holding us accountable. From our parental figures to teachers and coaches to employers and classmates.

Once we graduate college, suddenly we are supposed to be able to figure it all out on our own. *What gives?*

I say it's A-Okay for you to ask for help and get support for yourself, whatever that may look like for you.

There is no difference between you hiring a running coach to help you run a marathon versus hiring an accountability coach to help you stick to your habits and work through your limiting beliefs and patterns.

I chose to share my entire journey on social media to hold myself accountable, and you get to choose how you ask for help in your life.

# ACCOUNTABILITY BUDDIES FOR THE WIN

Today, I have daily support and get accountability in two ways:

- Friends who are accountability buddies
- Coaches who I invest in to help lead me toward the future I envision for myself

## ACCOUNTABILITY BUDDIES

I have a daily wins partner, Liz.

At the time of writing this, Liz and I have been sharing daily wins for nearly a year. We were in a high-level business coaching program together, and both of us were struggling with finding the wins in our day, so we decided to support each other in this habit.

Some days our wins are as simple as trying out a new restaurant and having a great meal, and other days it's celebrating an incredible launch for our businesses.

I also have my write-this-dang-book partner, Andi (pronounced AHN-di). Andi is another fellow coach, and we have become closer throughout the writing process.

When it came time to write this book, my book coach, Jake (more on him next), suggested I get an accountability partner for the writing process.

At first, I honestly almost didn't ask anyone. I had some limiting beliefs about how asking someone else to care about what I'm doing and making sure I'm writing my book was kind of selfish—people have better things to do with their time. I also figured I would share my progress on social media, just like I did 75 Hard.

I quickly realized that this was staying inside my comfort zone and playing small. It was time to take a dose of my own medicine and get uncomfortable.

I wanted to ask someone who I thought would help me take this seriously and really hold me to my word, someone who wasn't my usual go-to for stuff like this, and instantly, Andi came to mind.

She is so supportive and helpful and generous—and hilarious—in life. I thought it was an awesome opportunity to share this experience with a new friend and continue to build our relationship.

I can't imagine this journey without Andi by my "texting" side. Each night I shared with her not only that I got my writing done, but also what I was writing about. This often led to deeper conversation about the topic at hand (she is also a mindset coach), and I loved celebrating her wins with her as well.

## COACHING SUPPORT

I continue to invest in coaching because I'm betting on me.

Side note: I had a conversation with a friend today about Crypto investing. He was telling me about how great he was doing, and I was genuinely excited for him. As he was telling me how much he has been investing, I thought about how I was choosing to invest my finances these days. I've been investing in *me* — in my eyes, a sure thing.

This conversation brought up another mantra I repeat regularly:

- When you say *yes* to one thing, you are saying *no* to something else.

- When you say *no* to one thing, you are saying *yes* to something else.

By saying yes to investing in my growth and accountability with coaches, I'm saying no to investing in things like cryptocurrency.

But when I say no to investing in cryptocurrency, I'm saying yes to everything investing in coaches is giving me— the future and business and career I dream of.

Here's something to consider as you work through what accountability looks like for you: as I was talking with my friend, I realized that I'm really proud of the investments I've made in myself.

He is betting on Crypto, and I'm betting on me.

This is how I STAND IN MY POWER.

Currently, I have a team of four coaches I lean on for different aspects of my business:

**MINDSET:** I've told you about Nick, and he is probably the coach who knows me best. I can't tell you how many times I've snotty-nose-cried on the other side of the Zoom screen as he held space for me to work through my stuff. I don't know where I would be today if it wasn't for Nick's support and patience and belief in me.

**BUSINESS:** Jess (Glazer) DeRose is a friend-turned-coach and guided me through the process of creating The Aligned & Empowered Project and beyond. I've had her support as my business coach for several years, and I couldn't be more grateful for her guidance and support.

**BOOK:** Jake Kelfer is my book coach, and without him, you wouldn't be reading this right now. He kept me on track, helped me celebrate along the way, and held space for me when I needed to take more time to bring this baby to life. His wisdom and support was essential in my journey.

**NLP Practitioner Certification:** At the time of publication, Aimee Hennessey was my coach in Transcend Academy, where I was working to get certified in Neurolinguistic programming, EFT, Hypnotherapy, and T.I.M.E. Techniques. Aimee has been holding incredible space for me as I've worked through some of the most challenging months of my year, while teaching me new ways of coaching that I get to bring to my clients and beyond.

Through the years, I've had other coaches and friends who have had incredible influence in holding me accountable to my journey. My first business coach turned business therapist, Sarah Cook, played a major role in keeping me grounded and moving forward as I worked through 75 Hard and ultimately my dad's passing.

The men and women who I have gone through these coaching programs with have become some of my best friends, who helped keep me accountable and held space for me as needed every step of the way.

I also have a therapist, as I have mentioned, who keeps me in check in all the ways, helping with my mental health and beyond. Highly, *highly* recommend.

## RADICAL RESPONSIBILITY

Having accountability is taking responsibility for your actions and where you are currently at in life.

When you have an accountability partner or coach, you have someone helping you take *radical* responsibility for prioritizing something you may have otherwise deprioritized or ignored because no one was watching but you.

I say *radical* responsibility because true change comes when you take steps that are unlike any you may have taken before to own where you are at.

When my clients sign up to work with me, they are taking radical responsibility for their lives. This means they are taking action that is new, different, and likely outside their comfort zone, and could even be called extreme.

They are owning their life like they never have before.

Taking radical responsibility is their first step in STANDING IN THEIR POWER.

In NLP, we talk about living in *cause* over *effect* and how this is the true journey to empowerment.

Living in *effect* means we are constantly living as the victim of our circumstances—everything in our life is because of things outside of ourselves.

This puts us in a space of having zero control, living as the victim instead of victor.

It is true that there are things in life we have no control over. But living in *cause* allows us to take control of what we can control (sound familiar?).

This includes allowing ourselves to see the lesson or opportunity in the challenge before us. It also allows you the chance to step into your power and take control of an otherwise out-of-control situation.

Yes, accountability can be challenging—especially when *Matilda* (remember her?) is involved.

But, when you allow yourself the chance to have help in the form of accountability, you are letting yourself be seen by others and allowing them to show up for you as you would show up for them in return.

*This* is how you STAND IN YOUR POWER!

## DO THE DAMN THING

I want you to think of a daily habit you can start taking action on today. Who can you ask to be your accountability partner as you take on this new habit? How can you check in? A nightly text or sharing a story on Instagram and tagging them? If you are feeling super-sassy, make it public and share your journey with the world.

If you are an entrepreneur looking for a little support on a weekly basis, this process might be helpful for you and your accountability partner.

- Meet each week for thirty minutes
- Spend fifteen minutes for you, fifteen minutes for them
- During those fifteen minutes, you are concise and clear with the following update:
- What are you working on currently?
- What are your goals for the week?
- What are you thriving with?
- What do you need support with?

This is a great way to keep momentum going, and you can enjoy the process of building your empire with a fellow boss. Remember, a rising tide lifts all ships.

# SEVEN

# Celebration Is Key

"The more you praise and celebrate your life, the more
there is in life to celebrate."
—Oprah Winfrey

## THE MAGIC OF A WINNING STREAK

HAVE YOU EVER ...

Screamed as loud as you possibly could, at the top of your
lungs: "I'M ON A WINNING STREAK!"?

No?

Okay, well imagine if you did.

Not in the, "Eek I have to get escorted out of Starbucks
because I'm ruining everyone else's day" kind of way ...

But rather in a, "Holy shit, my life is so good, good things
keep happening to me all the time, every minute I'm lucky
enough to receive gifts of abundance, I'm one lucky SOB,
and I'm so excited I just can't hide it" kind of way.

Imagine what that would look like. What it would feel like to be constantly on a winning streak, every day, all day, and it can't be broken. How good would that be?

Now, you might be thinking, "Well, Charlie Sheen kind of ruined #WINNING for me, and I can't help but feel the yuck creep in when I say it."

I hear you. I feel you. I'm with you.

This is your invitation to own how winning feels for you, how celebration feels, and use it as a tool to help you STAND IN YOUR POWER.

At the THRIVE: Make Money Matter conference I went to back in May 2019 (where I was introduced to 75 Hard) I met one of the most inspiring speakers I had ever been introduced to.

His name is Charlie Jabaley (aka, Charlie Rocket), and his spirit, his joy, his *trust* that the Universe was on his side (and all of our sides) was infectious. I couldn't help but believe that he was right.

Charlie was a music executive who at a very young age helped build the hip hop community in Atlanta by managing the likes of 2Chainz and Travis Porter. He won Grammys and started clothing lines. He was a *very* successful entrepreneur.

But he was miserable.

At twenty-nine, he gave up his budding career, his millions in income, and his fame in the pursuit of joy and fulfillment and became a Nike athlete.

Since leaving the music industry, Charlie completed four marathons, an Ironman in New Zealand, and influenced how Nike defines athletes with the "If you have a body, you are an athlete" slogan.

Now, Charlie Rocket and the Dream Machine is dedicated to traveling across the country making dreams come true for underdogs from coast to coast.

At THRIVE, Charlie came onto the stage with two things:

- A book that looked like a spell book (he even referenced Harry Potter as he described it). It was his "magic, abracadabra, ask-and-it-is-given book"
- A bell, similar to what you would find on the counter at a store when you wanted to let someone know you were ready to check out

Charlie was a student and teacher of quantum physics and talked passionately about manifestation, the law of attraction, and how our number 1 priority should always be to live in a high-vibe state in order to attract high-vibe people, places, and things into our world. (Sound familiar? Charlie also knows that it's *good to feel good!*)

This is when Charlie introduced us all to the practice of winning streaks. This practice has become one of my favorite forms of celebration and gratitude, and I practice it with all of my clients every single day.

# I'M ON A WINNING STREAK

One surefire way to help you get from a low-vibe state to a higher-vibe state is to go on a gratitude rant. List out all the things that you are grateful for in this moment.

Raise your hand if your chest just got a little constricted when you read this because it's not that easy to find things to be happy about right now.

Raise your hand if you have a hard time celebrating wins because you don't want to make others "feel bad" that they don't have what you have.

Raise your hand if you have ever tried to go into a "gratitude rant" of some sort but felt blocked because from where you were sitting, there was nothing "big" happening to be grateful for.

I hear you. I see you. I'm with you. And I used to get stuck here too.

What I have learned is that gratitude isn't only about the things that are going right in your world, or about the big accomplishments, or about the moment your dreams finally come true.

Gratitude is about everything that *isn't going wrong* in your world.

It's important to dig in and get to the smaller stuff that often can get overlooked but would really make a difference if it wasn't available to you.

For example, right now I am very grateful for:

- Having ten healthy fingers (no sprains, hangnails, or paper cuts) that are allowing me to type this book right now.
- Having warm clothes to wear while I sit on my porch and watch the sun rise this morning (I wouldn't be able to focus if I was freezing).
- Having electricity so that I can power this computer and the lights so I can see what I'm doing (I probably would have broken a toe without it).

Charlie and winning streaks bring this concept of celebration to a whole other level.

Head over to www.MaryTheresaTringale.com/book to watch one of my favorite Charlie Rocket interviews where he talks about when he started implementing winning streaks into his every day.

For Charlie, he would acknowledge his winning streaks every day, everywhere, anytime, anyplace.

And his bell would anchor in the win.

He started winning streaks one random morning at Starbucks when he felt the need to be extra-grateful for the little things in his life.

When the barista told him his coffee would be $5, something anyone else might complain about being expensive, Charlie exclaimed, "All of that delicious happiness in one cup for only $5! Holy moly, I'm on a winning streak."

Charlie continued his winning streak that day by celebrating the small wins that don't get the attention they deserve, and he would ring the bell for every win:

- I woke up today—*ding*—Winning Streak
- I have clean water to drink—*ding*—Winning Streak
- I have an able body so I can walk outside—*ding*—Winning Streak
- I have a fridge full of food—*ding*—Winning streak

Side note: how cool would it be if we all had bells and it was a normal thing to ring the bell every single time you acknowledged a win?

You would be hearing bells all over the place. You would know people were consistently winning. It would be contagious and could raise the vibe for the entire community—heck, the entire world—if it was an everyday occurrence, don't you think?

The moral of this story is, if you can't show the Universe gratitude for the small things in life, you're saying you aren't ready for the big things.

Here is an example:

If you see a penny on the ground, what do you do?

Option A: Pass it on by, it's only a penny and might have some nastiness on it that no one wants to touch.

Option B: Pick it up and show so much gratitude to the Universe for literally dropping money in your lap, hug the penny, love on the penny, exclaim, "I'm so rich and abundant, I'm on a winning streak!"

Raise your hand if you chose Option A.

Yeah, it's okay, I get it.

But when you walk past that little penny as if it is nothing, as if it isn't enough to have your attention, you are signaling to the Universe that you aren't grateful for the small things, you aren't interested in what the small stuff (in this case, one cent) offers.

The Universe sees this as, "Well, if you aren't willing to celebrate the small, then you won't be able to handle the big."

I encourage you to consider picking up that penny next time and celebrating it with all the joy and gratitude you can muster.

Start showing gratitude for it all; start celebrating the smaller "in-between" moments just as often as the big stuff.

As Charlie's message of celebration really stuck with me after the THRIVE event, I realized that I myself had my own issues with celebration—and taking up space to do so.

I have no problem taking up space to ask important questions for things that I need answers to, like when I was in physics class or on a work meeting where I am responsible for delivering specific things.

If I'm not clear, I take up space and ask for what I need.

But when it came to celebration—especially of my own accomplishments—I hadn't stepped up to the plate.

I always waited for others to deem my accomplishments worthy of recognition.

If no one else told me my accomplishments were worthy of celebration, I assumed they weren't, so I didn't celebrate.

What a bunch of malarky.

Stepping into this space of consistent celebration, daily wins, and personal recognition for things as simple as not giving up has changed the game for me and so many of my clients.

Allowing ourselves the gift of celebrating where we are, where we have come from, and where we are headed is essential for growth.

Celebration could possibly be the most important tool in your toolbox. (I know I keep saying this, but I really, really mean it this time).

Raise your hand if you are still feeling squeamish about celebrating this because you don't feel like your friends, family, or colleagues will buy in and may judge you for it.

I see you. I hear you. And I'm here for you.

It can be hard to find spaces where we feel safe to celebrate it all, especially when our community or network or family or circle doesn't align with this practice.

That's why it's important to enlist a community that *does* celebrate it.

You can join a community (like The Aligned & Empowered Project) or create your own.

You are always welcome to share your wins in my world.

Your wins are my wins.

My wins are your wins.

A rising tide lifts all ships, so when you are in a high vibe, that helps me get there too.

I believe it is *good to feel good*, and in my space there shall be no shame around feeling good as often as possible.

And remember, I believe you should honor all the feelings, the high and the low.

Sometimes your win might be that you are feeling low, and that's okay. You spend time honoring those feelings, and you get to celebrate that too!

Let me be clear: I'm not advocating throwing your wins in someone else's face intending to make someone else feel bad for your wins and their losses.

Ain't nobody got time for that BS.

I'm saying to celebrate with intention that we live in an abundant space, where there is room for everyone to win, and that even on the days I'm not feeling so great, I get to raise my vibe by celebrating you.

So, to close out this chapter on celebration, I would like to share some personal wins with you.

- I am thirty-eight, single, A-Okay, and hitting my stride—Winning Streak
- After a few weeks of travel and holidays, I'm consistent again with my food intake and workout regimen—Winning Streak
- Today (as I write this) I am gearing up for the final coaching call of the fifth round of The AEP cohort, and this group has filled my cup so much, I'm going to truly miss our weekly calls so much—Winning Streak
- I am living in my dream apartment that I 100 percent manifested—Winning Streak
- I am surrounded by amazing, beautiful, encouraging people who lift me up and allow my light to shine—Winning Streak
- I am actively taking better care of my mental health and physical health than I ever have before—Winning Streak
- I am about to finish my first book—Winning Streak

Now, it's your turn.

**DO THE DAMN THING**

The time has come for you to celebrate your own winning streak. Do you need a safe space to share what is going on in your world, the moves you are making, the challenges you are taking on, the way you are facing fear each day? If you need this safe space, I got you. You can join us in our free Stand In Your Power Facebook group, you can email me or DM me on social media, or you can join the Aligned

& Empowered Project where wins are our currency. Whatever you need, I got you.

CELEBRATE, GIVE ME A WIN, LET'S RAISE THE VIBE TOGETHER.

Take up space.

Let your light shine.

STAND IN YOUR POWER.

Let's do this.

## You Still Got This!

Now that you know how to **BE, DO,** and **HAVE** it all, and have the tools to support your journey along the way, I wanted to spend the next three chapters sharing some words of wisdom, perspectives, and advice.

I share this with you from my own lived experiences. They are the ways in which I try and be every day, or, at least, as often as possible.

As always, take what works for you and leave the rest. I hope this information continues to support you as you continue your journey to living in your power.

EIGHT

# Go Your Own Way

"When women lose themselves, the world loses its way. We do not need more selfless women. What we need right now is more women who have detoxed themselves so completely from the world's expectations that they are full of nothing but themselves. What we need are women who are full of themselves. A woman who is full of herself knows and trusts herself enough to say and do what must be done. She lets the rest burn."
—Glennon Doyle, *Untamed*

## BE UNAPOLOGETIC IN THE PURSUIT OF GREATNESS

RAISE YOUR HAND IF YOU WERE BROUGHT UP BELIEVING that your life was supposed to look a certain way, by a certain age, with a certain job, with a certain household income, etc.

Raise your hand if you have felt pressure to put your desires, needs, or wants aside for the benefit of your significant other, children, friends, or coworkers because it is "better" to be selfless than selfish.

Raise your hand if you were told you were "too much" growing up; too bossy, too loud, too independent, too up in the air, too mellow, etc., and now you hide your natural tendency to live in your zone of genius because you are afraid of who may judge you for being you.

If you raised your hand to any of the above, I hear you. I see you. I'm with you.

This chapter is for you.

This chapter is me officially begging, pleading, wishing, hoping, praying that you will find a way to get out of your own way to own who you were meant to be so we can all benefit from your greatness.

This is your permission slip to do life whatever way *you* need to do it, so that you can live in your purpose, in your genius, as your most authentic self to light up the world.

This is me telling you it is okay for you to go your own way.

If you don't want to get married until later in life—do it!

If you don't want to have children—ever—do it!

If you want to focus on your career first and love and family second—do it!

If you want to be a nomad living paycheck to paycheck because that's what excites you and fills your cup—do it!

If you enjoy a simple, minimalistic life—do it!

If you want to get married young and have five children by the time you are thirty-five—do it!

If you want to break up with your significant other who is a beautiful human but isn't a good match for you—do it!

If you want to move to the other side of the world so you can experience a culture unlike your own—do it!

If you would rather invest in you instead of investing in Crypto because you really want to go all in on *you*—do it!

If you don't want anyone else to decide your worth, and you would rather go at it alone as a freelancer or entrepreneur—do it!

The time for you to create a life that works for you and your terms is *now*.

If you are living a certain way because someone else told you that this is the way you *have to* live, then you may be missing out on what your true calling is.

If you are feeling a nudge that something isn't quite right, or a whisper that you were meant for more, listen. That message is for you.

I have heard the whisper and felt the nudge that I was meant for a different life than the one I was brought up to believe I should want for a very long time.

I have basically chosen the opposite path of everyone else I grew up with and have been living a very different life than what a thirty-eight-year-old, cisgender, white, straight, female was "supposed" to be living.

The plan of:

1. Go to college
2. Get a job that pays the bills
3. Get a husband by twenty-six
4. Have children by thirty-one

went out the window as soon as I went to Emerson College in Boston. I was suddenly surrounded by a badass group of women who were unlike anyone else I grew up with. They were driven, determined, brilliant, and career oriented.

And they wanted BIG careers—living in NYC or LA. Two places I only dreamt of before.

Growing up, I didn't even know it was an option to work in Hollywood or for the magazine industry in NYC.

And yet, I found myself as an intern at Sony Pictures Television for a semester in LA and spent seven and a half years working in the magazine industry at both *Woman's Day Magazine* and *Men's Journal*.

This life of being so career-oriented was very different from the world in which I grew up, and having my career be my driver and "north star" is something I still look to even today.

I have personally never felt the pull, nudge, or calling to be a mother, yet. I know that someday I will be one, in some shape or form. But I have no sense that I'm supposed to be doing anything other than building my empire as an entrepreneur and coach (and now author!).

Sometimes, when I'm triggered by the expectations of what "should" have been, Matilda comes out to play. She asks silly questions like: "What's wrong with you that no one wants to marry you?"

or

"Time is a ticking. You're not a young chicken anymore. You are going to miss out if you don't prioritize romance and family."

or

"Maybe you should consider lowering the bar for the man you want in your life. Maybe it's time to settle for what you can get."

Thankfully, the one thing I have worked on mastering through the years is learning how to be so incredibly in tune with my inner wisdom that I never question if I'm exactly where I am supposed to be.

And I am so grateful for all the tools in my toolbox.

The walking, the journaling, the meditation, the accountability.

I can lean on friends and coaches and family to help me remember who the hell I am.

I am always able to jump back into my beingness and start taking aligned action that *feels good* and helps me have the life of my dreams.

And you can have this too!

This chapter is about embracing the thing inside of you that makes you, you.

It's about answering the call—your call—the desires and visions and talents that only you were given.

## ALIGNMENT FOR THE WIN

Do you know what happens when you risk doing anything other than going your own way?

You get out of alignment.

You know what happens when you get out of alignment?

Shit gets hard.

And not the "good" kind of hard that I love and encourage you to lean into.

I'm talking about the *unnecessary* hard that we create for ourselves because we are so stubborn and committed to being in the hardest place possible.

In *The Seven Spiritual Laws of Success,* Deepak Choprah speaks of the Law of Least Effort:

"Nature's intelligence functions with effortless ease . . . with carefreeness, harmony, and love. And when we harness the forces of harmony, joy, and love, we create success and good fortune with effortless ease."

This law essentially states that when we receive and accept life for what it is, receive the ebbs and flows, and not resist what is, success comes effortlessly.

When you are out of alignment, when you aren't living into your purpose, when you are too afraid to go your own way, you are missing out on the magic (and income, and opportunity, and prosperity, and abundance ...)

I had a conversation with one of the women in The AEP on a coaching call about how she had been struggling with her journey of going from corporate full-time work to successful entrepreneur and coach who owns her own business.

She had a *ton* of stories and excuses for why she was where she was, including that she feared she wasn't good at what she does (she is), that no one would say yes to her (not possible), or that she would get so successful it would all be taken away from her and she would be a complete failure (also not possible).

But all of this, we discovered, was masking the real reason she felt small: she was ashamed of the role she wanted to play in the world.

The truth was that *she* was judging who she was about to become if she stepped into the space of being a life coach. She felt shame that her natural calling to be a coach wasn't "prestigious" enough of a career, in her eyes.

It had nothing to do with fear of failure, or imposter syndrome, or even what other people thought of her—it was all her.

*She* was her own number one block and obstacle.

And until this conversation, she had no idea that she actually felt this way deep inside.

And you know what?

This amazing, powerful, hilarious, kind, loving woman is one of the best coaches I have ever met.

Her natural ability to empathize, support, and hold space for others is *incredible*.

When she would speak up on AEP calls to support the other women, I was always mesmerized by her insight and wisdom.

She was *born* to be a leader in this space.

But her own stories about how the title of "life coach" isn't a worthy enough profession was holding her back from offering her services to the world.

She was resisting her God-given gift, her natural desire, her calling, because she didn't think it was good enough..

When, in actuality, her living in her purpose is exactly the thing the world needs her to do most of all.

Luckily for all of us, this coaching session was a break-through moment for her, and hopefully she'll be getting out of her own way sooner rather than later.

My parting words for you here are this: The world needs you to do it your way. To live the life your heart is calling you to live. To allow, to stop resisting, to be your most powerful, authentic self.

Please oh please stop listening to what everyone else thinks you should do and start listening to what *you* think you should do.

We are so lucky to live in a day and age where we have the option of choosing our own life. Of knowing there are options, of being able to pivot when needed.

So, take advantage. Seize the opportunity. Don't sleep on this time of our lives.

Be you. The most beautiful, authentic, committed, real you. The world is counting on it.

## DO THE DAMN THING

Spend some time with your journal and answer these questions:

- What is the real block holding me back from living my truest life possible?
- How am I playing a role in the life I'm living, or not living, today?
- Am I living this life for me, or someone else?

These journal prompts may trigger you, so make sure you find a support to review them with, either an accountability buddy who can hold space for you, a coach, or a therapist. Remember, it's okay to ask for help when you need it.

# NINE

# The Ripple Effect

"Here is also a beautiful ripple effect that takes place when you love yourself. Your children learn how to love themselves; they teach their children how to love themselves and so on and so forth, and look at that, you have done your part to heal an entire lineage of people!"
—Rachel D. Greenwell, *How To Wear A Crown: A Practical Guide To Knowing Your Worth*

## THE 12 UNIVERSAL LAWS

Raise your hand if you have heard of the law of attraction or know of the book *The Secret* by Rhonda Byrne.

The Law of Attraction is one of the 12 Universal Laws that ancient spiritual teachers and philosophers believe to be unchanging laws that when you live with them, instead of against them, you can master your life with love and joy.

Charlie Rocket (Jabaley) talks a lot about quantum physics, which is the scientific proof behind the law of attraction and the law of vibration (why he believes so much in celebrating winning streaks nonstop) to raise your vibe and attract what you desire.

But what are these other Universal Laws? I'm so glad you asked!

Here is a very brief overview, but if you visit www.MaryTheresaTringale.com/book, I have some resources you can review to learn more.

1. **Law of Divine Oneness** We are all connected. Every thought, action, and event is connected to anything and everything else.
2. **Law of Vibration** At a microscopic level, everything is in motion (quantum physics), and our vibrational frequency can inform our lived experiences.
3. **Law of Correspondence** Everything happening on the outside is a reflection of what is happening on the inside.
4. **Law of Attraction** Like attracts like, and you have to believe that you are worthy of what you are seeking. If you believe you are only worth of receiving crap, you'll receive crap!
5. **Law of Inspired Action** Taking action based on the inner nudge you are feeling or hearing within. It's about allowing yourself to be inspired by your own thoughts and then taking action accordingly (this law relates to what we talked about in the previous chapter).
6. **Law of Perpetual Transmutation of Energy** Energetically, everything is constantly evolving and is fluctuating. Just as much as someone with negative energy can bring you

down, someone with high energy can bring
you up.

7. **Law of Cause and Effect** Every action will
   create an opposite and equal reaction. The
   reaction may not be in real time, but it will come
   back to you eventually. Karma.

8. **Law of Compensation** You reap what you sow.
   If you want something, you must contribute in
   some way toward getting it.

9. **Law of Relativity** Comparison doesn't matter
   because everything is neutral. Meaning comes
   down to our perspective and perception; we create
   our own values.

10. **Law of Polarity** Everything in life has an
    opposite. Good and evil, love and hate, warm and
    cold.

11. **Law of Rhythm** Cycles are a natural part of the
    universe. You can think of it as the seasons, that
    you are not always going to be the same,
    constantly moving through different times and
    seasons of life.

12. **Law of Gender** Energetically, everything has a
    masculine (doing) and feminine (being) energy.
    Historically, society has been very masculine
    (doing), which doesn't leave room for the feminine
    (being). Good thing we have learned in this book
    that it's essential to come from the feminine
    (being) *and then* lean into the masculine (doing).

## THE RIPPLE EFFECT IS REAL

Now that we have reviewed the 12 Universal laws, it's time
to talk about this thing we call the ripple effect.

This is what you will create for you and your world once you start prioritizing your needs, filling your cup, and listening to your intuition for guidance.

When we talk about the ripple effect, know that it's going to align with several of the Universal Laws, especially numbers 1, 2, and 6

1. **Law of Divine Oneness** We are all connected, your actions are in some way, shape, or form reaching me, affecting me, impacting me.
2. **Law of Vibration** The vibrational frequency you are putting out is having an effect on me in some way; I'm feeling it and connecting to it.
3. **Law of Perpetual Transmutation of Energy** The energy you are creating and putting into the world is transforming my energy in some way. It could be a big shift, or it could be a small shift—a shift it still is.

So, why is the ripple effect so important? Well, let's start with what it is in the first place:

According to Wikipedia: A *ripple effect* occurs when an initial disturbance to a system propagates outward to disturb an increasingly larger portion of the system, like ripples expanding across the water when an object is dropped into it.

The word I want to focus on here is *disturb*. "When an initial disturbance to a system propagates (spreads) outward."

When you start this process of BE-DO-HAVE, you are creating a new disturbance in your life. A disturbance to your nervous system, a disturbance to your energy, a disturbance to your belief systems, a disturbance to your physical body.

Disturbances are not always a bad thing, and hopefully in this case, if you embrace the process laid out in the previous chapters, it is a very, very good thing not only for you, but also the people in your life.

As the ripple effect progresses (in accordance with the three laws mentioned above), the disturbance you are creating is reaching the "larger portion of the system."

This might include your significant other, your family, your coworkers, your network, your community, and beyond.

The ripple effect that you get to create when you disrupt your ways of being and start introducing new habits, thoughts, and belief systems will reach far beyond what you can even imagine.

The most important thing to remember here is that you are *always* creating a ripple effect. Always. Whatever you are doing is disrupting the system and therefore disrupting the system of those around you.

What you are in control of is what your ripple effect ultimately creates.

Is it a ripple effect of positive change? Or is it a ripple effect of negative change?

What do you want to create for this world? (Great journal prompt.)

Understanding the importance of the ripple effect is really where it should all begin for you. I know you are someone who wants to make a positive impact on the world. I know you want to be helpful and supportive and leave the world a better place.

What I know for sure is that you aren't going to do it to your highest capacity by constantly prioritizing everything else besides yourself.

If you truly want to stand in your leadership, live in your power, and create a ripple effect of positive change, you must start with prioritizing *you* above all else.

Prioritize your mental health, your physical health, and all-around wellness. This BE-DO-HAVE process we have been working through is one way (the best way, if you ask me) to get there.

How do I know this works? Well, I am personally living this every day:

- I created a ripple effect when I started sharing my 75 Hard journey. I can't tell you how many people have tried it and changed their own lives because I stepped outside my comfort zone by sharing it all on social media.
- I created a ripple effect when I created The Aligned & Empowered Project. I tear up thinking about how the alumni are still creating their own ripple effects for their own worlds because of the work they did in this program.
- I create a ripple effect when I bring a vision to life through events. I believe that events are experiences that can change lives, and when I live into that philosophy, I create opportunity for others to change in ways I can't even begin to imagine.

But one of my most favorite examples of what the ripple effect can do when you start to take care of yourself is from one of the ladies of The AEP:

She is a mom who was struggling to keep her shit together when the COVID-19 pandemic first hit (as we all were), and she was especially struggling with keeping her son motivated with remote learning (as most parents—ahem, mothers—were).

She knew she needed to disrupt her system in some way and thought The AEP might be the best place to start (it is!)

She started with daily walks before joining The AEP and instantly saw a small shift and the benefit of the daily habit. It was evidence that she could, contrary to her previous stories and beliefs, maintain a habit for more than two days in a row.

Once she joined The AEP, she got into the work with journaling, showing up for coaching calls, and allowing herself to build awareness around the stories and agreements that didn't serve her so she could rewrite them to feel more empowered.

She started choosing herself daily in order to serve everyone else in her world. She created a ripple effect and soon saw the changes it was creating for others in her life.

- She had more patience and confidence at work, which helped manage her stress, and her students started to see better results. Ripple effect.
- Her relationship with her husband was stronger than ever with clear communication and boundaries. In fact, he was so inspired by the work

she was doing on herself, he started making similar changes in his own life. Ripple effect.

- Her son started to improve in school and advance in ways that even his teachers were surprised and inspired by. Ripple effect!

Never underestimate who is watching you take control of your own life. It isn't your job to worry about it, but don't sleep on the fact that someone is always watching.

Instead of worrying about how a person watching is judging you, focus on how your actions are inspiring them to do the same. How would you BE then?

Coming from this place of being, this place of creation, is how you STAND IN YOUR POWER and your leadership.

Be the influence you want to have on the world; the rest will follow.

## DO THE DAMN THING

Spend some time with your journal and answer these questions:

- What kind of a ripple effect do I want to create in the world?
- How can I show up for me *first* today?
- Who is watching me be me?
- Who do I want to impact with my actions today and in what way?
- What is the legacy I want to leave in this world?

Any "Aha!" moments? Share them with me on social media—this is the stuff I live for!

# TEN

# When in Doubt, Get Back to Basics

"Every action you take is a vote for the type of person you wish to become. No single instance will transform your beliefs, but as the votes build up, so does the evidence of your new identity."
—James Clear, *Atomic Habits*

## BACK TO THE VERY BEGINNING–A VERY GOOD PLACE TO START

AT THE TIME OF WRITING THIS BOOK, WE JUST (LAST NIGHT) wrapped up the fifth round of The Aligned & Empowered Project (lovingly referred to as AEP5). These ladies were a powerful crew, with major "Aha!" moments, massive movement toward leveling up, newfound inner peace, and an understanding of what it means to do the work.

Each graduation call is generally filled with moments of reflection and celebration for the journey the ladies took during their time in The AEP.

I like to begin each grad call the same way, with an epic dance party followed by a reminder that in or out of The Aligned & Empowered Project, the work continues. They are by no means "done" with the journey of self-discovery and growth.

I remind them that no matter where life may take them next, as far as their mindset work is concerned, they can count on always finding another layer of the onion to peel and always discovering something new about their beliefs, agreements, or fixed mindset that they didn't know existed before.

My advice is always the same, and it is the final piece of advice I'll share with you as we come the end of our time together in this book.

When you find yourself out of alignment, questioning your direction, or wondering what to do next, the answer will always be the same: *go back to basics and start again.*

1. Identify the person you want to BE.
2. DO the habits and practices that will get you there.
3. Open your arms, receive, and HAVE it all.

One of the guest coaches I asked to join us to help close out the second round of The AEP was my friend Brett Eaton, another mindset and high-performance coach. His message on this coaching call was the same as above but using this metaphor: What happens when you lose your keys? You go back to where you had them last. The same goes for when you lose your way or find yourself out of alignment, *go back to where you had "it" last.* ("It" being alignment, joy, purpose, vision, clarity, etc.)

In other words, choose your Identity Statement, create aligned habits, lean into the tools we've discussed in this book, and receive, receive, receive.

## PROOF IS IN THE PUDDING

A funny thing happens each time I wrap up another round of The AEP or start to launch the next cohort of participants.

Without fail, I'll get a DM, an email, or a text with a special message from an alumna of The AEP that generally brings me to tears.

The sender may have graduated from The AEP six months before, a year before, or eighteen months before. No matter how long the time has passed since they first said *yes* to The AEP, the message is generally the same:

*I have some big news to share, and it is all thanks to the habits and mindset work we did in The AEP.*

Here is a special text I woke up to one morning from AEP alumni Angelica as I was closing out the launch of The AEP5 over the summer:

*"I hope that it's not too late to be texting, but I wanted to let you know that I've been thinking about you these past several days. Starting on Monday, I decided to recommit to my habits. I feel that they gave me such a good anchor and guide, and although I'm generally good, I've felt something missing. Thank you for teaching me that I can always return to the good things that were working for me in order to help find my way!! I love you!"*

Here are a few of the other incredible wins The AEP alumni have shared with me since we began in May 2020:

- Buying their dream home
- Getting a much-deserved promotion
- Moving to a new city or state
- Finding their dream job (that they didn't even know existed)
- Getting engaged
- Increasing sales in their business by 200 percent
- Being accepted into graduate school
- Starting a new small business
- Getting pregnant
- Losing weight
- Starting their own group coaching program
- Leaving a toxic job
- Leaving a toxic relationship
- Moving in with their significant other
- Being accepted into nursing school

And I reiterate, these are results that came six to twelve months or more *after* their time in The AEP. But each of these results, as I was told via email, DM, text, or voice memo, were directly related to the work they continued to do long after their time working with me came to an end.

It was because they continued to dig in and stay committed to who they wanted to be. They had a vision for their life, and if they got lost along the way, they went back to where they last had the keys: they got back to basics, leaned into their tools, and started again.

One thing I can guarantee to you is that life is *full* of highs and lows—and you need the lows to understand how amazing the highs really are.

The good news is that the more you practice the tools I have shared with you and the more you lean into the discomfort and discipline needed to stay consistent with habits and do the mindset work, the quicker you'll move through the lows to get to the highs with celebration every step of the way.

My wish for you is that eventually the **BE-DO-HAVE** lifestyle is your norm, and prioritizing your own well-being above all else in order to create the ultimate ripple effect is your ultimate non-negotiable.

This book is a resource, one I hope you'll return to time and again. Whenever you wonder what to do next or whenever you are in need of a reminder of who the hell you are, flip through these pages, choose your own adventure, try a new tool or practice that you haven't tried before, and let the process do its *thang*.

The truth is, you have everything you need to move forward and through within you. These tools, practices, tips, and advice are here to help you discover it all.

## I NEED YOU, WE NEED YOU, THE WORLD NEEDS YOU

My final message is this.

Please, for the love of all things good and holy, get out of your own damn way. I need you. We need you. The world needs you to **STAND IN YOUR POWER** and be the person you were born to be. Please take action—aligned, beautiful, true action—that will help you be this person that the world needs you to be. Then, open those arms and receive, judgment-free (or as much as possible). Let the world show up for you, let me show up for you. See what happens next.

Now. Go.

## DO THE DAMN THING

It is now your turn. Go back through this book and start from the first DO THE DAMN THING way back at the end of chapter one. Don't skip out on this. This process, if you lean in and do it like your life depends on it, will change your life. If you decide on day one it isn't going to work, then you will be right. Allow, receive, believe. You got this my friend, and I'm cheering you on every step of the way.

Love,

M-T

# Acknowledgments

I want to give a big thank-you to everyone who helped me get to this very moment in my life as I complete this book and look forward to the process of bringing it to life for the world.

Currently, I am staring at a blazing fire in my fireplace, in the living room of my dream apartment that I manifested for my life. Outside, the world is white and covered in snow with our first real snowfall of the winter season. I couldn't have gotten here, to this exact moment, without the following people:

All the members of The Aligned & Empowered Project: You have all made my dream come true. Every time you posted your wins, shared your gratitude, showed up on calls, and made me laugh and cry, you were igniting a light within me. Please keep sharing your journey with me, please keep sharing your light with the world. Please, keep going.

Jake Kelfer, thank you for believing in me and helping me through the process of bringing this book to life. You went first and then shared your wisdom with the world. We are all better for it. I'm especially grateful for the patience you had with me through the process of getting this book to print. Your generosity with your time and support won't ever be forgotten.

Jess (Glazer) DeRose: thank you for being such a damn badass and letting me be a part of your journey. Your vision, skills, and support created the space I needed to not only bring The Aligned & Empowered Project to life, but also introduced me to Jake. I literally wouldn't be here without you.

Courtney Tucker: you, too, helped me bring my vision of The Aligned & Empowered Project to life. You believed in what I had to offer and helped me get my thoughts onto paper and sell it to the world. I'm so very grateful.

To my E+mpower family: those in the spring class of 2020 and those that have followed, you cheered me on as I welcomed the first seven ladies into The AEP. We did our money magnet dances, and we made massive impact in the world. Let's keep going!

Nick Pags: I'm so eternally grateful for the never-ending support you show me on a daily basis. We have become family since we first met in April of 2019, and where in the world would I be today without you. I am a better coach because I get to be a part of your world. Thank you for having me.

Sarah Cook: Thank you for being my support system through one of the hardest times of my life. The way you held space for me, becoming more my therapist than business coach, will never go forgotten. I am so grateful for you.

Michell, Jill, Ashley, Arielle, Bea, and Melissa: how lucky are we to have each other. I 100 percent wouldn't have made it to this point without you. I'll never forget how fate brought us together and how our desire to make the world a better place keeps us in each other's lives. May we have retreats together forever, "shaking it off" until we physically can't dance any more.

My Emerson Girls: our friendship has been the greatest gift and blessing in my life. Thank you for always being there for me, for keeping me laughing, and inspiring me to create a space where women can come together and celebrate the highs, lows, and everything in between. And thank you for the dancing. Always the dancing.

Andi & Liz: thank you for being my accountability buddies throughout this process. Liz, thank you for celebrating daily wins. And Andi, thank you for saying yes to keeping me accountable to writing this book. It was a joy to share the process with you and to allow our friendship to grow.

To my Momma Lorraine, the strongest, smartest woman I know. I hope this book makes you proud. Please don't tell me if you find any spelling or grammar errors. I love you.

Tom & Vin, I love you forever and ever, and also, just do what I'm telling you to do. K. Thanks.

Ashlynne, Arya, Emma, Isla, Desmond, Matteo and Leo: this book is for you. I hope you always find ways to STAND IN YOUR POWER, lean into your purpose, and find a way to leave the world a better place.

Gina & Holly: my sisters from other misters, I love you, I love you, I love you. There are no words for how very grateful I am to have you both in my life and on this journey with me.

Daddy: thank you for always believing in me. For encouraging me to be the boss that I am. For always making us laugh until your dying day. I miss you, I love you, I wouldn't have been able to do this without you.

# About the Author

Photo credit Share the Soul Photography

Mary-Theresa Tringale—Mary or M-T, for short—is an accountability and high-performance coach who loves nothing more than cheering others on. After her own radical transformation in 2019, M-T launched her coaching business with her signature program, The Aligned & Empowered project in 2020, to coach others through their own breakthroughs to find their true life's purpose.

After taking a leap of faith, M-T moved from the Boston area to New York City and landed what turned into a nearly eight-year career in the magazine publishing industry. M-T again picked up her life and moved to "the other Portland" in nearby Maine with nothing but faith that her next big move was destined for her there—and she was right. Since 2014, M-T has worked full time in marketing and events, and most recently found her true calling in launching her coaching business. She wants to remind others that they are not alone in their journey and are already equipped with everything they need to stand in their power.

Today, M-T is still on her journey of growth and expansion right alongside her clients. She holds a BS in marketing communications from Emerson College, and when she's not making earrings (@iamauntiemary on Instagram), Mary can be found moving outdoors—walking, skiing, or kayaking—and spending time with her friends and family, especially her nieces and nephews.

facebook.com/marytheresa.tringale

instagram.com/mary.theresa.tringale

tiktok.com/@mary.theresa.tringale

linkedin.com/in/marytheresatringale

Made in the USA
Middletown, DE
06 September 2023

37850181R00086